WORLD AT WAR
WORLD WAR TWO

WORLD AT WAR
WORLD WAR TWO

DUNCAN HILL

PHOTOGRAPHS BY
Daily Mail

Trans
Atlantic
Press

Published by Transatlantic Press in 2011

Transatlantic Press
38 Copthorne Road
Croxley Green
Hertfordshire, WD3 4AQ, UK

Design by John Dunne

A catalogue record for this book is available from the British Library.

ISBN 978–1–907176–68–5
Printed in China

Contents

Introduction

A mere 20 years after the Treaty of Versailles had, supposedly, drawn a line under 'the war to end all wars', the world was consumed by an even bloodier global conflagration. The 1919 treaty imposed swingeing terms on vanquished Germany, leaving it emasculated and humiliated; a nation seething with discontent, an economy crippled by hyper-inflation. Adolf Hitler, an Iron Cross-winning soldier in the 1914-18 conflict, was among the embittered. He blamed the Jews for all ills, and brought his warped views on racial purity into the political mainstream when his Nazi Party gained power in 1933.

Hitler dreamed of a glorious, 1000-year Reich. Territorial gains in Austria and Czechoslovakia were never going to sate his militaristic desires, a forlorn hope Britain and France still cleaved to at the beginning of 1939. Winston Churchill, then on the political sidelines, was one of the few siren voices warning of the Nazi threat. When Germany turned its expansionist gaze on Poland on 1 September 1939, war was inevitable. A vindicated Churchill emerged from his 'wilderness years' to head the Coalition Government. His stirring speeches helped boost morale, even as the German Army cut a swathe across Western Europe, with Britain the final prize. The situation became even more perilous as Mussolini's Italy weighed in on the Axis side just as the Battle of Britain was about to begin in the summer of 1940.

America played a pivotal role. Its Lend-Lease arrangement kept the Allies well supplied; in the Atlantic Charter Churchill and US President Franklin Roosevelt expressed their shared principles and goals, which could only be implemented 'after the final destruction of the Nazi tyranny'; Roosevelt fully backed the Manhattan Project, America's atomic weapons programme; and following the attack on Pearl Harbor in December 1941, the Axis now had to contend with the mighty US military machine.

The Allies prevailed, and the 'broad, sunlit uplands' of victory and freedom became a reality after six years of bloodshed. The battle was won first in Europe, when the full horrors of the Nazi death camps were revealed; then in Japan, after President Truman sanctioned the use of the atomic bomb on Hiroshima and Nagasaki. The obliteration of those cities helped make this the first war to claim more civilian than servicemen's lives, over 50 million fatalities in total.

World at War: World War Two uses contemporaneous reports and photographs from the *Daily Mail* archives, including many eyewitness accounts, to show how the conflict developed, describing the key battles, tactical decisions and turning points that settled the outcome.

LEFT: In October 1942 aboard a US aircraft carrier in the Pacific, scout aircraft and dive-bombers, tightly packed together on deck, are re-fuelled and re-armed, ready for attack on the Japanese.

The rise of Hitler

The end of the First World War had not really brought about any improvement in the level of tension between nations; it had simply changed the nature of the grievances and added some new ones. After the war, hopes for future peace in the world had been enshrined in the League of Nations, created to provide for a policy of 'Collective Security', but there were some doubts about how effective it would be, doubts which were to be fully vindicated.

Adolf Hitler had first come to public attention in 1923 when he made an unconstitutional attempt to seize power in Bavaria, known as the 'Munich Putsch'. It failed and he was sent to prison for nine months as a consequence. While imprisoned, he used the time to write *Mein Kampf* (My Struggle), which became his political programme. He claimed that Germany had not really been defeated as such in 1918, and that both the apparent defeat and the post-war settlement had been a betrayal, for which he blamed the Jews. One of the consequences of the Munich Putsch was that Hitler was now determined to seek power by legitimate means, as far as that was possible. Following his release in 1924, he reorganized his political party, creating what was in effect a private army. This paramilitary organization was known as the SA (Sturmabteilung), and by 1927 there were over 30,000 people in it. They were the 'Brownshirts', who intimidated their opponents and instigated violent conflicts with both Communists and Jews. In the meanwhile, the economic situation went from bad to worse.

ABOVE: **Nazi supporters line the streets of Weimar during Hitler's visit to the town in July 1936.**

RIGHT: **Crowds fawn upon Hitler as he attends Labour Day celebrations in Berlin's Lustgarten in May 1934.**

OPPOSITE LEFT: **Upon becoming Chancellor, Hitler set about consolidating his power. He had his closest rivals murdered on the 'Night of the Long Knives' in July 1934.**

OPPOSITE RIGHT ABOVE: **Hitler poses for a photograph with a Polish delegation led by Poland's Foreign Minister, Colonel Joseph Beck. One of Hitler's first foreign policy achievements as Chancellor was to conclude a Non-Aggression Pact with neighbouring Poland.**

OPPOSITE BELOW LEFT: **German soldiers marching at a military parade in Berlin in 1935.**

OPPOSITE BELOW MIDDLE: **Hitler addresses a crowd of Hitler Youth at the annual Nazi Party Congress in Nuremberg.**

OPPOSITE BELOW RIGHT: **German troops in Berlin swear an oath of allegiance to Adolf Hitler in 1934.**

The Great Depression

In October 1929, a contagious outbreak of panic selling on the New York stock exchange – which had previously been booming – resulted in the Wall Street Crash. This financial disaster wiped millions of dollars off the value of shares and reverberated on the global economy as a whole, ushering in the Great Depression. The economic collapse had an enormous impact throughout Europe, but was most severe in Germany, where the government was completely dependent on American finance. The value of the mark fell swiftly and catastrophically, unemployment soared and, not surprisingly, discontent spread. In this atmosphere the more moderate and democratic political parties were unable to provide any solutions to the problems besetting the nation. People began to turn to the extreme parties of the right and left in increasing numbers, and unrest and violent street fighting became more common.

Nazi popularity grows

There were only 12 National Socialist members in the Reichstag, the German parliament, by the start of 1930. However, as the Great Depression set in, support for the Nazis skyrocketed. They won 107 seats in the elections of autumn 1930, becoming the second-strongest political party in the Reichstag. Hitler stood for the presidency of Germany in 1932 and won more than 13 million votes, placing him a close second behind Paul von Hindenburg, the great general of the First World War. Parliamentary elections that year saw the Nazis becoming the largest single party in the Reichstag.

Alarmed at the rapid rise of Hitler and his party, a group of Conservative politicians persuaded President Hindenburg to appoint Hitler as Chancellor. They hoped that they could control Hitler by bringing him into the establishment and separating him from his party.

The Führer

However, the Nazis continued to expand their influence. Chancellor Hitler blamed the Communists for an arson attack on the Reichstag building in February 1933. This certainly boosted support for the Nazi party in the March 1933 elections, and allowed them to achieve an overall majority in parliament.

Hitler used his small majority to pass a law giving him power as Chancellor to govern without the consent of the Reichstag. President Hindenburg died in August 1934 and Hitler seized the opportunity to combine the two offices of the Chancellor and the President in one new role. He was now in control of the armed forces and called himself by the title 'Führer', the leader of all the German people. All German servicemen had to swear an oath of personal loyalty to him.

Appeasement

While he consolidated his power inside Germany, Hitler moved cautiously in his foreign policy. He signed a non-aggression pact with Poland and agreed to negotiate with European powers over disarmament. However, from 1934 he secretly began rearming Germany so that it would become strong enough to achieve his main foreign policy goal: the reversal of the Treaty of Versailles.

As the 1930s progressed, the German military grew stronger and the international situation became ever more favourable. The failure of the League of Nations to tackle both Japanese aggression in Manchuria in 1931 and Italian aggression in Abyssinia in 1935 made it obvious that the organization would not seriously challenge Hitler's attempts to reverse the Treaty of Versailles. The ineffectiveness of the League revealed that the Great Powers were distracted and indifferent. The United States, Britain and France were still grappling with the Great Depression and Stalin was busy purging and collectivizing in the Soviet Union.

Reoccupying the Rhine

In 1936, Hitler decided to test the waters and send troops into the Rhineland, which had been established as a demilitarized zone under the terms of the treaty. His officers had been instructed to withdraw should they encounter any resistance. However, there was no response from the Great Powers, and an emboldened Hitler began building a line of fortifications along the French and Belgian borders.

Austria was the next country to attract his attention. The Treaty of Versailles had decreed that Austria and Germany should never be united. Austria was, however, in chaos – much of it caused by Austrian Nazis – and Hitler used this as a pretext for sending the German army into the country. On March 13, 1938, his troops marched into Vienna and Austria was integrated into the Reich. Hitler, himself an Austrian, returned in triumph to the capital where he had lived in poverty before the First World War.

Next on Hitler's agenda was Czechoslovakia, a democratic country that had been created by the Versailles Treaty. Some three million Germans lived in Czechoslovakia, mainly in a region along the German border called the Sudetenland. Hitler insisted that this region should be absorbed into the Reich.

ABOVE RIGHT: **Hitler follows his army into Linz, Austria to oversee the 'Anschluss', the Union of Austria and Germany, in March 1938.**

ABOVE RIGHT INSERT. **Neville Chamberlain returns home waving a 'piece of paper' signed by Hitler promising a peaceful resolution to European disputes in future. Chamberlain declared that he had returned bringing 'peace with honour, peace in our time.'**

ABOVE: **American President Franklin Delano Roosevelt pictured in his home in Hyde Park, New York in 1938. The United States stayed out of European disputes while it tried to rebuild its battered economy in the 1930s.**

BELOW: **Hitler's position was further strengthened in May 1939 when he signed an alliance, 'The Pact of Steel' with Mussolini.**

The Munich Agreement

These demands caused concern in London, but Britain was in no position to challenge Germany in Central Europe. The British military was greatly overstretched across the vast Empire and the public had no appetite for a new European conflict. Instead, the British Prime Minister, Neville Chamberlain went to Germany to negotiate with Hitler. At their meeting in Munich on September 29, 1938, Hitler and Chamberlain agreed that the Sudetenland should join Germany, but that this would be Hitler's last territorial demand in Europe. Chamberlain returned, claiming he had secured 'peace for our time', but his critics labelled this as 'appeasement'.

In March 1939, under the pretext of unrest in Slovakia, Germany occupied the rest of Czechoslovakia. The Munich Agreement was in tatters and the British public were outraged. Hitherto, many people had believed that Hitler's demands had been reasonable, but overt aggression in Czechoslovakia was a step too far, and the public called for firm action. In response, the British government issued guarantees to protect Poland, Romania and Greece against German aggression.

ABOVE: **Hitler and Chamberlain meet at Bad Godesberg in Germany on September 23, 1938, where Hitler detailed his demands for the Sudetenland. Chamberlain spent the week convincing the Czechoslovak government to agree the terms before signing the Agreement with Hitler in Munich a week later.**

ABOVE RIGHT: **Hitler congratulates his Foreign Minister, Joachim von Ribbentrop, upon his return from signing the Nazi-Soviet Pact in Moscow.**

BELOW: **Hitler salutes as he walks through a sea of flowers in the Sudetenland, October 3, 1938.**

TOP RIGHT: **Joseph Stalin, leader of the Soviet Union, pictured at a conference in January 1938. In the late 1930s, Stalin was preoccupied with industrial development, agricultural collectivization and purging Russian society of 'saboteurs'.**

The Nazi Soviet pact

The British government began preparing for a war during 1939 by speeding up programmes of rearmament and civil defence. However, the government's inherent anti-Communism meant that it was slow to develop ties with the Soviet Union, which was vital if Germany was to be threatened with a two-front war. Given the violent ideological differences between the Soviet Union and the Nazis, the British believed that Stalin would inevitably support a war against Hitler and did very little to strengthen relations. The announcement on August 23 that Germany and the Soviet Union had signed a non-aggression pact came as a complete surprise to London. The pact was expedient; Hitler avoided a two-front war and Stalin avoided a war he was not yet ready to fight. A secret clause of the pact also promised Stalin a free hand in the Baltic states and in eastern Poland. On September 1, 1939, with his Eastern Front secure, Hitler risked war in the West by invading Poland.

Occupation of Czechoslovakia

Hitler's plans to make Germany the ruling power of Europe started with pulling in the ethnic German peoples that lived in the nearby states of Austria, Bohemia, Moravia and Czechoslovakia; with the people came their territory. After moving first on Austria in March 1938, Hitler's ultimatum regarding the other Sudeten territories led to their annexation under the Munich Agreement negotiated with Britain and France in September 1938.

In March 1939, events reached their inevitable conclusion: however willing and able to resist Nazi aggression, Czechoslovakia would not go to war without support from Britain and France who maintained their course of appeasement. Hitler forced a bloodless surrender by Czechoslovakia and brought some of its territories under control as German Protectorates. The rest of the country was gradually broken up, with Hungary and Poland both acquiring territory. As with all his treaties and agreements, Munich was a device to buy time and to allay the suspicions of his opponents.

Although the break-up of Czechoslovakia was achieved by political means, a government in exile was formed and many Czechs fled to serve with Allied forces; an active resistance was maintained through the war, notably assassinating Reinard Heydrich, Himmler's deputy and at the time the Protector of Bohemia and Moravia.

ABOVE: **A local girl in the newly-freed Sudeten areas fraternises with German soldiers after troops occupied the No.2 zone of the Czech Sudetenland in October 1938, in accordance with the recently agreed Four Power Pact.**

BELOW: **The inhabitants give a hearty welcome to German troops at Kleinphilipsreuth.**

British pledge to Poland is without reserve

The pledge: ... In the event of any action which clearly threatened Polish independence, and which the Polish Government accordingly considered it vital to resist with their national forces, His Majesty's Government would feel themselves bound at once to lend the Polish Government all support in their power. - The Premier in the House yesterday.

Britain has offered Poland a mutual anti-aggression pact to which other Powers will be invited to subscribe. It is hoped that Col. Beck, Polish Foreign Minister, will sign it when he comes to London next week. The pledge given by the Prime Minister in the House of Commons yesterday to support Poland if she is attacked was purely to cover an interim period following rumours - which have not been confirmed - of German troop movements.

Apparently the Cabinet thought that the situation in Eastern Europe was sufficiently urgent to justify a unilateral declaration by the British Government. Ministers were also becoming acutely aware of the necessity to give the country some idea of their intentions.

The pledge given by the Prime Minister goes far beyond any commitment entered into by Britain since the end of the Great War. It is meant to form the basis of a strong anti-aggression front, by which it is hoped to preserve peace.

The Prime Minister's pledge to Poland is without reservation. Contrary to assertions made in London yesterday, there are no British conditions regarding Danzig or the Polish Corridor.

ABOVE: Crestfallen men and women watched the Germans troops enter Prague on March 17, 1939.

LEFT: An elderly lady in Friedland presented German soldiers with flowers after General Von Book's troops crossed the Czech frontier at Rumburg and Friedland.

German invasion of Poland

In the early hours of September 1, 1939, German troops crossed the border into Polish territory triggering the largest war the world has ever seen. The Polish army, consisting mainly of cavalry divisions, was no match for the modern, mechanized German army. The Luftwaffe quickly won air superiority over the smaller Polish air force and began pummelling Polish cities. As Poland met its fate, frantic debates ensued in London and Paris over how to respond. By evening, the decision was made to issue an ultimatum demanding that Hitler withdraw promptly from Poland or face war.

The British and French Ambassadors handed the text of their ultimatums to the German foreign minister, Ribbentrop, who agreed to pass them on to Hitler. The British and French ultimatums expired at 11 a.m. and 5 p.m. on Sunday September 3 respectively. Neither country heard back from Hitler and consequently a state of war ensued.

ABOVE RIGHT: **Polish refugees stream out of Warsaw to escape the relentless bombardment.**

BELOW: **Hitler addresses the Reichstag in the Kroll Opera House on the day of the invasion of Poland. In the speech he blamed Poland for starting the war by firing upon German territory that morning. He** warned that 'whoever departs from the rules of humane warfare can only expect that we shall do the same'.

ABOVE: **Poles march through Warsaw on their way to dig trenches for the defence of the city.**

DAILY MAIL   SEPTEMBER 4, 1939

War 11 A.M., September 3, 1939

Great Britain and France are at war with Germany. We now fight against the blackest tyranny that has ever held men in bondage. We fight to defend, and to restore, freedom and justice on earth.

Let us face the truth. This was inevitable whether it began with Austria, Sudetenland, Bohemia, or Danzig. If it had not come over Danzig it would have come later upon some other issue. It became inevitable from the day Hitler seized power in Germany and began his criminal career by enslaving his own people. For his one aim since then has been gradually to enslave all others by the methods of brute force.

Once more Britain, her Empire and her friends are engaged in a conflict to uphold Right against Might.

If the democracies had flinched now, they would have been compelled to abdicate for ever their title to be called the champions of liberty. The fate of these small nations who have already lost their rights would have been theirs in turn.

This was the dominant thought in the inspiring message broadcast by the King to his people last night. We go to war because we must. In His Majesty's words: 'For the sake of all that we ourselves hold dear, and of the world's order and peace, it is unthinkable that we should refuse to meet the challenge.'

Stalin invades Poland

The Polish commander, Marshal Smigly-Rydz, hoped in vain that Polish defences could hold out until Britain and France attacked in the west. However, his men were sitting ducks for Germany's 'Stuka' dive-bombers, and Polish cavalrymen were gunned down with ease as they futilely tried to take on German tank units.

On September 17, Stalin moved his troops into eastern Poland to fulfil the secret clause of the Nazi-Soviet Pact. He disguised his land grab as a mission to liberate Ukrainians and White Russians from Polish domination. The Red Army encountered little resistance from the Poles who were completely tied up on the Western Front. On September 28, Ribbentrop met with his Soviet counterpart Vyacheslav Molotov to sign the German-Soviet Boundary and Friendship Treaty, which officially carved the spoils of Poland between them. There was some resentment among Germans that the Soviets were to be handed territory that had been won by the Wehrmacht, especially as Stalin waited more than two weeks before declaring war.

The fall of Warsaw

The Polish capital, Warsaw, held out for several weeks against the Wehrmacht, which feared that street fighting would be too costly. Instead, the German army besieged the city and then bombed it into submission. The devastating attacks resulted in thousands of civilian deaths and the destruction of the city. The troops defending Warsaw surrendered on September 27 in order to relieve the suffering of the city's civilian population, but the German occupation that followed was to make their lives much worse. Politicians, academics, soldiers and ordinary civilians were massacred as the Nazis immediately set about destroying any potential opposition. The Germans began to ethnically cleanse Poland by expelling the 'subhuman' Poles from their homes and sending German families to replace them. Exceptions were made for those who were deemed sufficiently Aryan and agreed to be 'Germanized'.

Polish Jews were singled out for the harshest treatment; they were subjected to barbaric attacks and forced to move to ghettos, cut off from the outside world. However, this was only to be a temporary arrangement, and Poland's Jewish population was to suffer even worse when the Nazis decided upon their 'Final Solution'.

ABOVE LEFT: **Polish POWs line up for food in German prison camps.**

ABOVE RIGHT: **Hitler observes the destruction of Warsaw from a hill overlooking the city.**

RIGHT: **German troops train in preparation for air raids after the Allied declaration of war.**

BELOW: **Polish troops wait for the Germans to arrive in Warsaw after the city's capitulation.**

The Evening News

LARGEST EVENING NET SALE IN THE WORLD

POLAND INVADED

Big German Offensive on the Corridor : Bombing Raids on Warsaw, Cracow and other Polish Towns

DANZIG ANNEXED TO-DAY BY PROCLAMATION

French Cabinet Met and Issued Order For General Mobilisation

HITLER AND ITALY: "I DO NOT APPEAL TO FOREIGN HELP"

PARLIAMENT SUMMONED FOR 6 P.M.

BRITAIN STANDS BY POLAND

Hitler—"Goering Is My Successor If I Fall"

Britain prepares for war

For the first few months, there seemed to be little change. In Britain, rationing began. A night-time blackout was introduced and children were evacuated from cities to the country – both measures designed to protect the country from German air raids, which were not to happen for another nine months. There were, however, some raids on shipping by German submarines. A large French army and a much smaller British Expeditionary force maintained defensive positions in Northern France, preparing for the possibility of invasion. However, as the months passed, it seemed increasingly unlikely that Hitler would strike in western Europe, and talk of a 'phoney war' spread. Further to the east, though, the situation was different. During the period of the phoney war in the west, bitter fighting continued in Poland, Lithuania, Latvia and Estonia.

To Chamberlain:-

KILL NAZISM FOR EVER

WE'RE ALL BEHIND YOU

ABOVE: **Troops marching into Piccadilly Circus, London, in 1939.** Little funds had been made available for the military during the 1920s and 1930s and rearmament and civil defence programmes had to be rapidly stepped up after the Sudetenland crisis in 1938.

LEFT: **Shop signs supporting the government's declaration of war against the Nazi regime became commonplace.**

BELOW: **Children are taught how to use gas masks.** The British government feared the Germans would mount a gas attack and implored people to 'always carry your gas mask'. In the event the Germans never used of poison gas during their raids on Britain.

BOTTOM: **The statue of Eros at Piccadilly Circus, London, is boarded up to protect it from the impending air raids.**

War in Scandinavia

At the end of 1939 the Red Army invaded neutral Finland because the Finnish government had refused to accept Stalin's territorial demands. Helsinki was badly damaged by Soviet bombing raids, but the winter snow came to the aid of the Finns. Finnish soldiers used guerrilla tactics to slow and reverse the Soviet advance during December and January. The Soviets struck back with a major offensive in February, forcing the Finnish government to accept a punitive peace agreement.

On April 9,1940, Hitler launched simultaneous attacks against major ports in Denmark and Norway. There were some contingents from Britain and its Allies already in Norway, and these were rapidly deployed in defence. But the German command of the air – and a general lack of reinforcements, despite strong naval support – meant that the defenders were quickly forced to withdraw. There was one possible bright spot, though: the Allies had managed to inflict significant losses on the German fleet in the Norwegian campaign.

ABOVE: **Iron railings were removed from many public places such as parks, gardens and squares in order to be resmelted for use in munitions. Private owners were encouraged to do the same.**

RIGHT: **Signposts and street names were removed across Britain in case they assisted invading German troops.**

BELOW RIGHT: **British Boy Scouts collect waste paper as the country embarked on a recycling drive.**

BELOW: **Sandbags being filled in Hampstead. They were used to protect buildings across the country.**

Evacuating the cities

As the most likely targets of German bombing raids, London and other major British industrial cities began to see the mass evacuation of schoolchildren to rural areas from September 1939. For many children it would be the first time they had been separated from their families, and would certainly be the first time that most would spend Christmas in unfamiliar surroundings.

BELOW: Carrying their gas masks in cases and wearing luggage labels to help identify them, this group of children from the Hugh Myddelton School in Clerkenwell were part of the first wave of evacuees who left London on the day Hitler invaded Poland, 1st September, 1939.

BOTTOM RIGHT: Children at Maryville Road School in Leyton escorted down to the school air raid shelter for safety. Initially, the new start of term had been delayed by many weeks, as schools could not reopen until they had their own air raid shelter. Schools were only allowed to teach the number of children for which the shelter could provide safety, often resulting in a part-time shift system with many limited to half a day's schooling.

BELOW RIGHT: A group of young children sheltering during an air raid at a school on the south coast; teachers used songs and comics to entertain them.

DAILY MAIL SEPTEMBER 2, 1939

"The children have all behaved marvellously"

The greatest organised movement of a human population in the world's history started yesterday. As if by some quiet smooth-working machine, nearly 1,000,000 children, mothers, blind and maimed people were taken from danger to safety. In three days - perhaps less - 3,000,000 will have made the journey across the invisible frontier. Thousands of households all over Britain yesterday welcomed small strangers who were to be for a time members of the family.

Most homes in the evacuated areas were adapting themselves bravely to a sadder change which had robbed them of their children. London has lost much of its laughter. Nearly half of the 3,000,000 are being evacuated from the Greater London area. The rest are from the naval and shipping areas and the industrial districts of the Midlands, North, and Scotland.

Everywhere the task of moving this enormous number of children was carried out with great ease, owing to the thorough preparation and the co-operation of officials, parents, and children. And officials everywhere said 'the children behaved simply marvellously.'

Seeking safety

In the first weeks of the war nearly four million people moved from evacuation to reception areas. These included pregnant women, mothers of pre-school children and disabled people, as well as school-age children. Throughout the war, evacuation schemes continued, with peak numbers related directly to the severity of the bombing. After the 'phoney war' of the first year, many children returned home, only to be re-evacuated when the Blitz began. Even before then, some children, evacuated to the south coast of England, had to be relocated when the area suffered attacks during the summer of 1940.

School-age children were evacuated without their parents. They were required to report to their school with only a change of clothes, basic toilet essentials, a packed lunch and, of course, a gas mask. At the school they were tagged with luggage labels, a precaution against children becoming lost but especially important for the youngest, who may not have known their address. Accompanied by teachers and helpers, the children were taken by buses and trains to the reception areas. Trips were as long as twelve hours; many children arrived exhausted by the journey, upset at leaving their parents and fearful of what life would be like in their new home.

TOP: **Initially, those who had been evacuated to coastal areas were able to enjoy their freedom playing on the beaches but this luxury was limited as gradually coastlines were covered in barbed wire to protect the public from mines.**

LEFT: **A group of British children wave goodbye to their families as they wait to board a train.**

ABOVE: **Even prior to the declaration of war, children began to be evacuated from areas most at risk of bombing. Schoolchildren such as these in Edgware were ferried by buses to railway stations.**

Recruiting a fighting force

Following the declaration of war there was an immediate need to extend the numbers of men in the armed services. In addition to regular soldiers, members of territorial reserve forces, volunteers and those who were conscripted prepared to be called up to serve as required. A Conscription Bill had been passed in May 1939, and soon afterwards all young men under 21 were registered. The following year, some 30,000 more were signed up.

ABOVE LEFT: Charles Remnant calls for volunteers to join the 'Citizen's Army' at a meeting held on Tooting Bec Common.

ABOVE RIGHT: Soon after the evacuation from Dunkirk, on June 22, 1940, 30,000 men registered for military service at labour exchanges throughout the country.

BELOW: The first batch of men aged 22, but not yet 23, report at various military centres for training, 15th January, 1940.

Defenders of the home front

Although its appeasement strategy prevailed until Germany's invasion of Poland, Britain had been preparing for possible war. As refugees from Nazi oppression steadily arrived on Britain's shores, the consequences of invasion could be seen immediately in Poland, where resistance failed under German tactics. Churchill proposed the formation of a defence force of 500,000 volunteers not deemed fit for military service but still able to fight. On 14th May 1940, Anthony Eden, Secretary of State for War broadcast to the nation inviting men to sign up for the Local Defence Volunteers. The bland acronym LDV and the problems of training and equipment held back its success. Churchill turned the situation around by renaming it the Home Guard in July. The Battle of Britain and the threatened German invasion made the Home Guard one more demand among many for training and equipment; the return from Dunkirk of thousands of troops minus their weapons made those combatants a priority and the role of the Home Guard was seen as secondary support. However by 1943, even though the threat of invasion had largely subsided, the Home Guard was more of a force to be reckoned with, numbering 1.5m armed and trained, with a plan of defence – from standing look-out for German paratroop attacks, to guerrilla warfare. The Home Guard was stood down in December 1944 finally disbanding in December 1945.

TOP: **Local Defence Volunteers (LDV) on parade. The LDV was set up as Germany unleashed its blitzkrieg in Europe. In July 1940 the LDV changed its name to the Home Guard, which later became affectionately known as 'Dad's Army'. Many of those who joined up were older but had seen action in the Great War.**

ABOVE: **Local Defence Volunteers march at a parade ground in Balham. They are weaponless but some have LDV armbands and soldiers' caps.**

BELOW: **The Citizen's Army hold their first parade on Tooting Bec Common, dressed in civilian clothes and 'armed' with sticks and umbrellas. It was intended as a defence force in the event of a German invasion.**

SEPTEMBER 12, 1939
Britain's troops in action on western front - official

British troops have landed in France and are in action alongside the French Army. They have taken part in the advances into German territory. This news was released dramatically at 9.35 p.m. yesterday by the Ministry of Information.

The transport of the B.E.F. has taken several days, and has been carried out successfully without the loss of a single life.

The despatch of the troops was carried out with the greatest secrecy, so as to reduce to a minimum the danger of attack by submarines or aircraft. A tremendous ovation was given by the French populace when the first soldier marched ashore - and the scenes recalled those of 1914. No details of the units or their positions in France can be given.

The fall of France

Just before dawn on May 10, the German assault on Western Europe finally began. In a swift and comprehensive move, soon to be widely known as blitzkrieg, German paratroopers and bombers successfully struck at positions in Holland, Belgium and Luxembourg, facilitating rapid infantry assaults deep into these countries. In response, the Allies committed a large part of their forces to Belgium.

The Germans advanced at speed through the Low Countries, aiming to cut the Allied forces in two and push many of their troops towards the coast. At the same time armoured Panzer divisions broke through the French lines at Sedan. They stormed across northern France, heading towards the Channel coast within a matter of days. There was comparative chaos in the Allied forces; the speed and scope of the assault had stunned everyone. Their troops in the north, now successfully caught in the German pincer movement, began to retreat towards the Channel ports, notably to a perimeter around Dunkirk. A huge evacuation from France was authorized on May 26. This evacuation would be the first test for Winston Churchill, who had replaced Neville Chamberlain as Britain's Prime Minister sixteen days earlier; Chamberlain had finally resigned following severe criticism over the government's response to the German advances in Norway and Denmark.

TOP: **French soldiers march towards the front line. Germany unexpectedly invaded France through the dense forest of the Ardennes region of Belgium, and in doing so, circumvented France's heavily defended 'Maginot Line' fortifications along the German border.**

ABOVE: **French troops take aim at German positions from the first-floor windows of a ruined house in a village near the Belgian border. The French military censor forbade the publication of the name of the village.**

LEFT: **More troops rush up a rickety stairway to man the first-floor windows, while their** commanding officer issues orders from a niche in the wall in the right of the picture.

BELOW: **With fierce fighting occurring on the other side of the building, French troops run from house to house to take up more positions in a desperate attempt to stem the German advance until reinforcements arrived.**

Dunkirk

In the event, the evacuation, codenamed Operation Dynamo, was an enormous success. It had been thought that some 45,000 Allied troops could be rescued from Dunkirk – but 338,226 men were rescued from the beaches between May 26 and June 4, in often appalling conditions. There were many naval ships, but the evacuation was marked by the use of hundreds of small ships – whatever vessels were available on the south coast of Britain. The weather, by and large, was favourable and the RAF were also able to help, but the evacuation beaches were under almost constant attack. Dynamo was a success in terms of the sheer number of lives saved, but thousands of vehicles, weapons and tons of supplies were left behind.

The Vichy government

Hitler had now succeeded in gaining control of the Channel coast, and the rest of France was soon to fall. The German army entered Paris some ten days later, on June 14 – just a month after the initial attacks on the country. Italy entered the war in support of Hitler, and by June 22, with all of northern France occupied by German troops and columns advancing southwards towards the border with Spain, the French Premier, Marshal Pétain, agreed to an armistice with Hitler. Under its conditions, France had to disarm and was to be divided into two basic sections. The northern zone and the northern and western coasts were under direct German control, but the southern part of the country would be governed by a collaborationist government led by Pétain and based at the spa town of Vichy. By the end of June the British-owned Channel Islands, so close to France, had also fallen to Germany.

TOP RIGHT: **French tanks on manoeuvres in January 1940. This period was known as the 'Phoney War' because both sides had declared a state of war existed, but neither side had launched an attack.**

MIDDLE RIGHT: **French soldiers return from manning border** posts during the 'Phoney War' period.

RIGHT: **Reservists dig air-raid shelters in Paris in September 1939.**

ABOVE: **Paris experiences its first air raid, September 1939. There was relatively little aerial bombardment of the city in** comparison with other European capitals.

BELOW: **Columns of Allied soldiers await evacuation from the beach at Dunkirk.**

The Battle of Britain

Most of Western Europe was now under Hitler's control, but Britain remained a serious obstacle to his ambitions. He set his sights on invading the country, and developed a plan called Operation Sea Lion. In order for this to be successful, however, the Germans had to effectively control the Channel and subdue Britain's south coast. As a result attacks were initiated, both on the sea and from the air. Shipping convoys were the first victims, and then, by August 1940, attacks began on the vital airfields of southern England. This was the start of the Battle of Britain.

OPPOSITE: An aerial view of the Luftwaffe flying over Britain.

OPPOSITE ABOVE LEFT: Britain's new Prime Minister, Winston Churchill, visits Ramsgate, one of the most heavily affected areas of Britain during the Battle of Britain in 1940.

OPPOSITE ABOVE RIGHT: A German plane plummets to the ground over Sussex in August 1940.

OPPOSITE BELOW RIGHT: Squadron Leader Douglas Bader had a distinguished career as an RAF pilot, despite having lost both of his legs in a crash in 1931.

ABOVE LEFT: Much of the Battle of Britain was confined to the southeast of England. However, German fighters menaced the skies all over the country. This reconnaissance plane was brought down in Scotland.

MIDDLE LEFT: Vapour trails mark the scene of a dogfight between the RAF and the Luftwaffe. Curious civilians often came onto the streets to watch and cheer on the RAF.

BELOW LEFT: Bren gunners kept a watchful eye on the skies over Britain.

BELOW: A squadron of Hurricane fighters fly in close formation. Along with the Spitfire this aircraft was the best defence Britain had against the Luftwaffe.

DAILY MAIL JUNE 19, 1940

The Battle of Britain

The Prime Minister gave the House of Commons last night 'some indication of the solid, practical grounds upon which we are basing our invincible resolve to continue the war.'

The professional advisers of the three Services, he said, unitedly advised that we should do it and that there were good and reasonable hopes of final victory.

In this island there were now over 1,250,000 men under arms, backed by 500,000 Local Defence Volunteers. We might expect very large additions to our weapons in the near future. And, 'after all we have a Navy, which some people seem to forget.' Our fighter air strength is stronger at present in relation to Germany's than it had ever been.

'The Battle of Britain' said Mr. Churchill, 'is about to begin. On this battle depends the survival of Christian civilisation. I look forward confidently to the exploits of our fighter pilots, who will have the glory of saving their native land and our island home from the most deadly of all attacks.

'There remains the danger of the bombing attacks, which will certainly be made very soon upon us by the bomber forces of the enemy. It is quite true that these forces are superior in number to ours, but we have a very large bombing force also, which we shall use to strike at the military targets in Germany without intermission.

'What General Weygand called the Battle of France is over. The Battle of Britain is about to begin. On this battle depends the survival of Christian civilisation. Upon it depends our own British life and the long continuity of our institutions and our Empire. The whole fury and might of the enemy must very soon be turned upon us. Hitler knows he will have to break us in this island or lose the war. If we can stand up to him all Europe may be freed and the life of the world may move forward into broad, sunlit uplands. But if we fail, the whole world, including the United States and all that we have known and cared for, will sink into the abyss of a new dark age made more sinister and perhaps more prolonged by the lights of a perverted science.

'Let us therefore brace ourselves to our duty and so bear ourselves that if the British Commonwealth and Empire last for a thousand years, men will still say, "This was their finest hour."'

Goering's four-day promise

Hitler and his blitzkrieg commanders were understandably confident about their war machine but Nazi hubris bred false assumptions that would lead to Germany's unexpected defeat in the Battle of Britain. The Luftwaffe had dominated the skies of Western Europe during the blitzkrieg; its task now was to crush the RAF and disable its aircraft production. Field Marshal Hermann Goering, the Luftwaffe commander, boasted that the RAF would be broken in four days and its production capability wiped out in four weeks. However, the RAF were not to succumb to Goering's plan; the Battle of Britain was to have four clear phases and on June 18, Churchill predicted Britain's struggle for survival with his famous 'Finest Hour' speech.

LEFT: RAF pilots sleep and play games in their rest room at their base 'somewhere in Scotland'.

BELOW: Fighter pilots leap into action and rush to their planes after a warning from HQ that an unidentified plane had been spotted by the Observer Corps.

ABOVE: The overwhelming speed of the German war machine as it moved west, and Prime Minister Chamberlain's general failure to effect any resistance, frustrated Winston Churchill. In the years before the war, Churchill was critical of Chamberlain's lack of preparation against the obvious rearming of Germany by Hitler's Nazis. On May 10, Chamberlain resigned and recommended Churchill as the man to head an all-party war government. He accepted the invitation from George VI and immediately stepped into the role, much to the relief of the nation. On May 13, his first great speech to Parliament sounded around the nation with the immortal words "I have nothing to offer but blood, toil, tears and sweat."

ABOVE RIGHT: In April 1940 Winston Churchill paid a visit to one of Britain's dockyards, the primary targets for Luftwaffe bombers. Addressing the assembled workers, he questioned, 'Are we downhearted?' to be greeted with a resounding, 'No!' This was a catchphrase from a song that was used throughout the Battle of Britain and the Blitz.

BELOW RIGHT: Adolf Hitler in conference with Reichsmarschall Hermann Goering (2nd left), commander of the Luftwaffe. Hitler made him personally responsible for defeating the RAF prior to Operation Sealion, the planned invasion of Britain in September 1940.

JUNE 11, 1940
Italy: hostilities open

Hostilities between Italy and the Allies began at midnight. New York reports that Italian troops invaded the French Riviera at 6.30 last night were emphatically denied by a Government spokesman in Rome.

Signor Mussolini has chosen the crucial hour in the great battle for France to take his momentous step, but Britain and France have long been prepared to meet such a situation. It can be assumed that Britain will quickly take the offensive at sea. Her naval dispositions in the Mediterranean and other preparations have been made with the object of aiming swift and heavy blows at Italy.

A few days ago the British Government, in agreement with the French, decided to impose the full force of contraband control on all Italian ships. Italian shipping at Malta was seized early this morning. All Italians on the island were rounded up.

Rome radio announced that Signor Mussolini will be Supreme Commander of Italian armed forces, "although the King of Italy still remains the nominal chief." Marshal Badoglio has been made Commander-in-Chief of the Army.

Mr. Churchill will make a statement on the new situation to-day.

Heavy German losses

The summer of 1940 was balmy, with many days of sunshine. Aircrews fighting for their life one moment could be recuperating at the margins of their grassy runways soon after, ready at an instant to return to battle. However, the weather wasn't good the whole time. At the beginning of August, Eagle Day - the day the Luftwaffe began its real assault on the RAF - was quite seriously delayed by bad flying conditions, finally launching in earnest on August 13, after low cloud cleared in the early afternoon. Confusion in the German command made the planned attack less effective; the Luftwaffe were surprised by the firm resolve and force of the defending RAF who lost 13 aircraft in the air compared with 47 German planes.

Non-stop production lines

The Minister of Aircraft Production was in charge of the Ministry of Aircraft Production, one of the specialised supply ministries set up by the British Government during World War II. As the name suggests, it was responsible for aircraft production for the British forces; primarily the Royal Air Force, but also the Fleet Air Arm. The department was formed in 1940 by Winston Churchill in response to the production problems that winning the Battle of Britain posed. The first minister was Lord Beaverbrook and under his control the Ministry presided over an enormous increase in British aircraft production. Lord Beaverbrook, pushed for aircraft production to have priority over virtually all other types of munitions production for raw materials. In 1940 Britain produced in excess of 15,000 aircraft, 4,000 more than Germany.

LEFT: A production line for the Miles Master, one of the RAF training aircraft.

BELOW: A Spitfire production line. Whilst the Hurricane was more numerous, and accounted for more German losses than the Spitfire, the speed and agility of the Spitfire made it a formidable fighter plane.

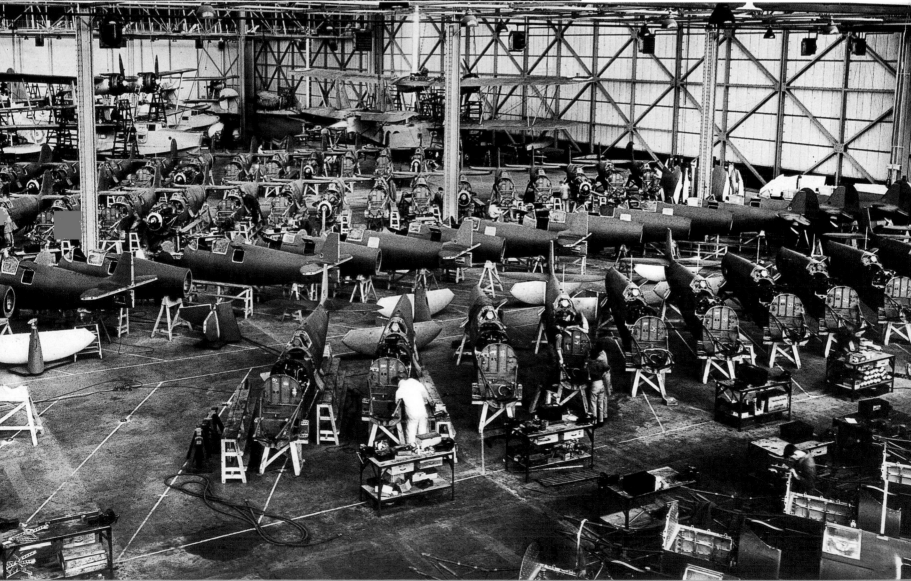

ABOVE: The limitations of the Bristol Blenheim led to the development of the Beaufort, which entered service with a Coastal Command squadron In 1940. Just over 2,000 were built with the bulk of production at Blackburn's Yorkshire works. The light bomber was intended to carry torpedoes to be used against the German navy and in aerial mine-laying as well as short-range. From July 1940 to the end of the year, Bomber Command lost nearly 330 aircraft and over 1,400 aircrew killed, missing or PoW.

LEFT: The Spitfire, designed by R. J. Mitchell and powered by a single Rolls-Royce engine, could fly at high or low altitudes, was able to evade most enemy fighters and also performed valuable reconnaissance work. During the war 'Spitfire Funds' were set up, when groups would fundraise for a Spitfire to be manufactured. This was combined with public collections of donated metal such as aluminium pans. By the close of the war 20,351 planes had been produced for the RAF.

FAR LEFT: Amongst the most outstanding RAF pilots during the Battle of Britain was James 'Ginger' Lacey, who shot down more German planes than any other pilot, with a total of eighteen.

LEFT: Bader, having just received the DSO pictured with Pilot Officer W.L. Knight (right) and Flight Lieutenant G.E. Ball.

BELOW: Bader (centre) surrounded by fellow officers and crew. In 1941 he had to bail out over German-occupied France and was placed in a prisoner-of-war camp. After repeated attempts to escape he was sent to Colditz and finally freed by the U S Army in April 1945. Despite his request, he was not able to fight in the remainder of the war.

Hitler abandons 'Operation Sealion'

On September 7, the new German approach ushered in the fourth and final phase of the Battle of Britain with the beginning of the Blitz as 950 German aircraft attacked London in the first and last massed daylight raid on the capital; 300 civilians were killed and 1,300 seriously wounded. For the next 57 consecutive days, London was remorselessly bombed in night raids. Fighter Command was amazed at this development, which perversely saved it from destruction, allowing its forces to recuperate and airfields to be restored. It was a terrible price for Londoners to pay, the death toll rose to 2,000 by September 10. However, September 15 marked the heaviest bombardment of the capital so far – but at a cost to the Luftwaffe of 56 planes. This date, originally designated as the launch for 'Operation Sealion', would prove a turning point in the Battle of Britain, as the German High Command realised that their invasion of Britain would be at an unsustainable cost. Thus, September 15 became Battle of Britain Day. On September 17, Hitler abandoned 'Operation Sealion' but not until October 29 could Britain breathe a little easier as the stream of German raiding aircraft subsided.

ABOVE: **Members of the Women's Auxiliary Air Force (WAAF) in training. Although women did not fly combat missions, the contribution of women in the auxiliary services was invaluable. The WAAF staffed radar stations whilst, amongst other duties, the women in the ATS manned anti-aircraft guns, and those of the Air Transport Auxiliary flew missions delivering new aircraft.**

LEFT: **Shipping and submarine movements are tracked in the control room of RAF Coastal Command, which provided aerial protection of Allied shipping from both the Luftwaffe and German U-boats. It received much less glory than its Fighter and Bomber Command cousins. In the first phase of the Battle of Britain, the so-called 'Kanalkampf', from July 10 to August 11, Luftwaffe attacks focused on shipping in the English Channel and the North Sea.**

BELOW: **Women of the Auxiliary Territorial Service (ATS) on observation duty at an anti-aircraft battery. Although they didn't handle the armament they were trained to use the rangefinders and accurately identify enemy aircraft.**

Counting the cost

The milestone date for the end of the Battle of Britain – October 29– was arbitrary to some extent as Britain would continue to experience the German Blitz until the early summer of 1941. Nevertheless, at this point in the war, it was possible to begin counting the cost of this decisive battle: during the Battle of Britain from July 10 to October 31, Britain lost 1,065 aircraft (including 1,004 fighters) and 544 pilots; German losses numbered 1,922 aircraft (including 879 fighters, 80 Stukas and 881 bombers). British civilian losses in the Blitz that ended in May 1941 soared to over 40,000 killed and 50,000 injured. German Luftwaffe losses from August 1940 until March 1941 were nearly 3,000 aircraft lost and 3,363 aircrew killed, with 2,117 wounded and 2,641 taken prisoner.

BELOW: As this picture shows, RAF pilots needed considerable stamina: sorties might begin at dawn with an adrenalin-fuelled run to their aircraft, laden down with their flying equipment. At the peak of the Battle, they would continue flying sorties as long as they could keep awake and had an airworthy machine. They were known to bale out of a doomed plane, be picked up and then immediately return to combat. Many in their crippled aircraft preferred to glide to earth in forced landings, especially when over the Channel.

RIGHT: Only one member of the four-man crew of this Heinkel bomber survived when it was brought down on a night mission at the beginning of September.

AUGUST 16 1940
London's First Air Raid

German dive-bombers swooped on Croydon Aerodrome last evening in the first bombing raid in the London area. One bomb hit an aerodrome building and there were some casualties, but there was little damage in the town. At least one 'plane, swooping over the streets, machine-gunned groups of civilians, but there were no serious casualties.

It was London's first real air raid, and the fifth alarm of the war. Sirens were sounded all over London, the alarm lasting for only a few minutes.

Heinkel twin-engined bombers, escorted by Messerschmitt fighters, came over and divided into two sections to attack. They were met by terrific anti-aircraft gun barrage, and fighters went up to intercept them.

At least three Germans were brought down over and around Croydon, and others were destroyed on their way home. One came down in a wood and was burned out. One of the crew, caught in a tree by his parachute ropes, shook hands with his captors when released.

Several 'planes swooped to within a few hundred feet of the streets and machine-gunned civilians. A Mr. Green and his wife and children were machine-gunned as they ran to their garden shelter, but none was hit. Mrs. Green had her baby in her arms.

ABOVE LEFT: The kills tally on this shot-down Bf 109 gives an indication of RAF losses and the performance of the German fighter plane. In the early days of the war the Bf 109 clearly had an advantage over the British machines, especially the many outdated craft that were deployed in France.

ABOVE: The stove in this airmen's mess provides the warming focal point for the pilots. Their inertia belies the squadron's energy - they had a tally of 60 Luftwaffe kills by the end of 1940.

TOP: Battle of Britain aircraft flew at great height with unpressurised cabins. In from 16,000 feet oxygen was required to maintain consciousness, the cockpit would become very cold and ice could impair the mechanics and cloud the plexiglass. To combat the intense cold, the parachute manufacturer Leslie Irvin devised the characteristic airman's jacket from very supple sheepskin, tailored to give maximum warmth whilst allowing freedom to move. The aircrew also wore fleece-lined boots and gloves.

Blitz on Britain's cities

Even though the invasion of Britain was called off, Germany continued to bomb Britain's cities in the hope of breaking civilian morale. The Blitz began in September 1940 with attacks on London. Civilian targets were struck across the city from the docklands in the east to Buckingham Palace in the west. Londoners were especially vulnerable because few people had space for air-raid shelters. Consequently many people crammed into underground Tube stations. These undoubtedly saved many lives, but were not without risk. On October 14, 1940, sixty-four people were killed at Balham Tube station when a bomb hit a water main, flooding the station.

Britain had been prepared for such an aerial bombardment since the beginning of the war, and many targets had been anticipated. The country had made provision for air raids: blackout conditions were imposed at night, air-raid shelters had been built, and there had even been a mass issue of gas masks, on the assumption that Hitler might make use of chemical weapons. Although poison gas was never used in the Blitz, casualties were high as densely populated areas were subjected to sustained bombardment. Though a lot of children had been evacuated to the countryside from the cities at the start of the war, most of them had returned during the period of the 'phoney war', and many of them died.

ABOVE RIGHT: **Civilians** shelter during an overnight air raid in the relative safety of Holborn Tube station. Few people in London had space at their homes for an air-raid shelter so many crowded into Underground stations. The government assisted them by putting bunkbeds and latrines in the shelters.

ABOVE: **An anti-aircraft battery at work during a raid on the north of England.**

BELOW RIGHT: **A tramcar destroyed during a daylight raid in Blackfriars Road.**

BELOW: **St Paul's Cathedral stands shrouded in smoke after a major air raid on London on Sunday December 29.**

First strikes

London was the focus for most Blitz attacks. At first, the Germans mounted sorties day and night but losses were large and after a week the Luftwaffe switched most of their operations to take place under cover of darkness.

LEFT: On the fifth night of the Blitz, East Enders used Liverpool Street and aother underground stations to try and escape the bombing raids

BELOW LEFT: Urban bombing destroyed hundreds of homes and businesses, leaving many civilians homeless and shops and services wiped out. However, people had little choice but to adjust to these challenging circumstances and most did so well. Provisions were made for the homeless, with buildings such as schools being used as temporary accomodation.

BELOW: A British soldier, heavily laden with equipment, pauses for a mug of tea at a London station.

LEFT: Temporary Post Offices were designed to be portable and could be erected swiftly in order to replace Post Offices which had been damaged by bombing.

ABOVE: Women and children queue for food at a communal cooking centre set up by the London Council.

BOTTOM: This street fruit seller boasts that his oranges have come through Musso's (Mussolini's) 'Lake' – a nickname for the Mediterranean. He also has bananas for sale – a rarity during the war, especially by the time of the Blitz.

Bombing of Coventry

The Blitz was widened beyond London and the industrial city of Coventry was targeted on the night of November 14. The city's weak defences offered little opposition to the Luftwaffe, allowing them to utterly devastate the city centre, causing great loss of life. The German tactic was to drop incendiary devices to start fires that would continue to wreck the city long after the bombers' departure. A long list of other cities followed suit. Britain's seaports and shipyards at Southampton, Liverpool, Bristol, Portsmouth, Plymouth and Glasgow were subjected to particularly severe raids. The raids petered out after the Germans invaded the Soviet Union in June 1941 and the Luftwaffe was redeployed east. By this time, tens of thousands of civilians had been killed and hundreds of thousands had been made homeless. Although Germany would continue to bomb Britain intermittently, the worst of the raids were over for British civilians. However, for the German civilians, the Blitz had barely begun.

TOP: Liverpool suffers a pre-Christmas raid on December 21, 1940.

ABOVE: A row of taxis destroyed by bombing in London's Leicester Square.

RIGHT: The ruined city centre of Coventry still smoulders after the air raid on November 14, 1940.

LEFT: Firemen tackle a blaze at a factory in Birmingham after a raid in November 1940.

DAILY MAIL NOVEMBER 16, 1940

Homes for all in smitten city

Coventry, hard-smitten by as heavy a night of bombing as even London has suffered, has shown itself to-night as a city of good Samaritans. Throughout the suburbs and the city the well-to-do and the poor alike have thrown open their houses to the homeless. Hundreds of men, women, and children whose homes were wrecked 24 hours ago have been welcomed to-night in those of people they had never seen before.

In working-class districts particularly I saw hastily scrawled notices in the windows of house after house: 'Room for two,' 'Room for three,' 'Will take four children.' No one who knocked at these doors was refused admission. People who had lost everything were told by complete strangers, 'You're welcome to share everything we've got.'

The aftermath of death and suffering has been a wave of warm humanity. In schoolrooms, empty mansions, and church halls, the homeless have gone to sleep to-night. 'No one is without a bed, and no one has gone to sleep hungry,' a city council official told me. 'It's marvellous the way people have rallied round.'

As the people were preparing their makeshift accommodation gunfire was heard again to-night. But Coventry went on with the work of restoration. I saw men and women still living in the wrecks of their homes. On houses whose roofs had been blasted away the people had rigged makeshift covers. 'Hitler?' said one

housewife to me. 'No fear! We stay put. And we're going to go on sleeping here.'

A pall of smoke hung over many areas of Coventry to-day. Two thousand high-explosive and thousands of incendiary bombs were rained indiscriminately on the city last night in a dusk-till-dawn air raid. Main streets were reduced to acres of rubble, and famous public buildings, cinemas, shops, houses, were obliterated. A thousand people were killed and injured and thousands more found themselves without homes. Yet the spirit of the people is unconquerable.

Only a shell of walls remains of Coventry's famous cathedral. Churches, public baths, clubs, cinemas, hotels, and hundreds of shops and business premises have been damaged. In the suburbs hundreds of houses have been demolished and thousands of people made homeless. The attack lasted eleven hours. It is estimated here that at least 100 'planes, arriving in waves, took part. The first raiders to arrive dropped incendiary bombs, and many fires were started. As the intensity of the attack grew, the din became terrific.

There are no greater heroes in the city now than the staff of a hospital which suffered a direct hit. The operating theatre was wrecked, but to-night doctors and nurses who have been working throughout last night and to-day are still on duty tending the wounded people being rescued from the debris.

The King and Queen stay at home

Lowering public morale was a key aim in the German High Command's bombing strategy and it proved to be a frightening experience for many, and affected everyone's life. Nevertheless, while every member of the population was touched in some way, they did not become demoralised. In fact, the constant attacks seemed to provoke the reverse effect to that intended – the sense of a nation pulling together, for bombs did not discriminate, no one, not even the King and Queen who remained in Buckingham Palace for the duration of the war, was spared the effects or the fear.

LEFT: A crater just outside the gates of Buckingham Palace was one of five, all caused by bombs dropped near to each other in September 1940.

BELOW: Workmen labour to repair one of the areas of damage.

BOTTOM: Winston Churchill joined King George VI and Queen Elizabeth to inspect some damage in the grounds. The culprit was a time bomb dropped by a German raider. The area affected was part of the building adapted to provide a swimming pool for Princess Elizabeth and Princess Margaret.

TOP: A policeman shows off some of the wreckage caused by the bomb that destroyed the Palace's North Lodge.

ABOVE: The North Lodge, next to Constitution Hill, received a direct hit in a raid in March 1941. A policeman died when one of the stone pillars fell on him.

RIGHT ABOVE AND BELOW: Following a night of heavy bombing the Queen toured the East End, visiting the site of a bombed hospital and speaking to local families.

SEPTEMBER 12, 1940

Buckingham Palace hit by bomb

Buckingham Palace has now shared with Britain's humblest homes the fury of the Nazi raiders. Yesterday I walked round the gardens with Sir Alan Lascelles, the King's Assistant Private Secretary, and saw the effects of a time bomb which landed 6ft. from the Palace.

It exploded early on Tuesday - during another raid - wrecked part of the Princesses' swimming pool and smashed nearly every window in the north wing, including the windows of the royal suite.

The King and Queen spent the week-end at Windsor, but when the King returned to London yesterday he, the Queen, and Mr. Churchill, who lunched at the Palace, inspected the crater and also the damaged part of the Palace.

No one was hurt. Members of the household had been moved to another part of the Palace when the bomb was discovered near the Belgian Suite.

250-pounder

The windows of the King's and Queen's bedrooms and dressing-rooms; the Queen's bow-windowed sitting-room and the King's little balconied work-room were blown out. Showers of soot, glass and masonry poured into these rooms, covering the floors with thick dust and chipping walls and doors. The bomb - believed to be a 250-pounder - buried itself 10ft. deep, forcing up stone slabs on the terrace.

It demolished one wall of a Georgian-period building which was converted into a swimming pool about two years ago. This had previously been a conservatory.

The explosion broke in pieces some of the huge columns of the building. Masonry, weighing many tons, was flung into the air. Some of it was hurled over roofs and landed in the quadrangle. An underground shelter underneath the pool was also damaged.

Legacy of the bombing

Following the Fire of London raid, the capital suffered almost nightly bombing until May 1941. During the night of May 11 over 500 Luftwaffe planes dropped hundreds of high explosive bombs and tens of thousands of incendiary devices. Many important London landmarks were damaged that night, including the chamber of the House of Commons and Big Ben. This was the last great bombing raid on London, but one of the legacies of the months of sustained bombing, was the fear of the attackers returning.

LEFT: The Lord Mayor of London spent New Year's Day 1941 inspecting the damage in Aldermanbury.

BELOW: The Guildhall suffered severe damage during the raid. Here, wreckage of the roof beams lies in the Banqueting Hall. It was to take years of careful restoration work post-war to return the building to its former glory.

LEFT: The scene at St Bride's Street in London after a raid. The majority of the people were on their way to work and would need to salvage what they could from the premises and find alternative places to work.

BELOW LEFT: A quick and effective method for the police to give the 'All Clear'.

BELOW RIGHT: The Pioneer Corps was formed to help with clearance and salvage operations with the workers largely drawn from the unemployed. The Salvation Army was again on hand to provide food and drink for them.

RAIDERS
PASSED

MAY 12, 1941

Biggest London raid

It had been a fantastic night. London was bathed in the golden glow of the full moon. Soon the mingled incendiaries and explosives turned parts of the city into an inferno. Rolling billows of smoke blotted out the moonlit sky.

Some commercial buildings were hit. But once more it was the houses of the people, rich and poor, that suffered most.

Over all was the roar of the guns, the whistle and crump of bombs, and the crackle of the fighters machine-guns high in the sky. Five hospitals were hit and there were casualties at three of them. One was a children's hospital.

At one hospital four wards were demolished, and twelve people, including a night sister and a woman dispenser, were killed. A sister saw the bomb tear its way through her ward and then explode in the one beneath. She at once started rescuing 18 men patients who were buried under the debris. With the help of nurses, she got them all out except one, who was killed.

Nearby, an earlier bomb had hit an A.R.P. rescue party depot. Two men were killed and six injured. Those who escaped had just finished extricating their colleagues when the hospital was hit. They immediately ran to the spot and helped nurses who were struggling with huge pieces of masonry beneath which some of the patients were trapped.

Women left the shelter in a block of flats to help the men fire-watchers and to salvage furniture when the roof of the flats was set on fire by incendiary bombs. They formed human chains to pass buckets of water for the stirrup pumps.

There was heavy loss of life when a bomb crashed through the roof of a London hotel and exploded in the basement, in which many of the 140 guests and employees were sheltering.

There were other casualties at a shelter, a rest centre, and a warden's post and a street market, where people were trapped. A cinema and several churches were struck. A club and an A.T.S. post also received direct hits.

BELOW: **Young women pick their way through the debris after the the last major, and most devastating raid on London.**

RIGHT: **A postman tries to deliver letters in Watling Street, London.**

ABOVE LEFT: Men at work in the torpedo workroom.

ABOVE RIGHT: Shells arriving in the shell-inspecting shop at an ordnance factory.

LEFT: Inspection was carried out at all stages of production. Here the casings for naval shells are checked.

BELOW: Inspecting shells at a Royal Ordnance factory. Quality control was very important in order to prevent the military being put at risk from its own equipment.

Munitions

Once the government had established a military force, its next priority was to organise the production of the munitions with which that force could fight the war. Factory space, a labour force and raw materials were needed to produce weapons in large quantities. Some raw materials were imported but many were provided by 'salvaging' or recycling items already in the country. Teams of women and children, organised by the Women's Voluntary Service (WVS), toured from house to house, collecting metal in the form of tin baths, saucepans and old tin cans. Additionally, they collected scrap rubber, rags, waste paper and old animal bones, all of which had some use in the production of weaponry.

ABOVE RIGHT: **Thousands of empty cartridge cases ready for filling.**

ABOVE: **A factory inspecting room which was 'working at emergency pressure, day and night, to produce small arms, spare parts and tools.' Britain had not spent money on armaments in the years after the First World War and consequently, when war broke out again, it was a race to provide the equipment the military needed.**

BELOW: **Every torpedo was 'tried out' and 'passed under working condition' before being dispatched to a Royal Navy ship.**

Lend-Lease

At sea, the Battle of the Atlantic was underway. It was vital that Britain could continue to be supplied by sea; the country's survival depended upon it. The essential convoys of supplies were under constant attack from both the Luftwaffe and U-boats, which were now able to operate from bases along the coastline of France, much extending their range. Most of the supplies came from the United States, but their cost was beginning to prove prohibitive to Britain's straitened wartime economy. President Roosevelt was willing to give any support short of actual military involvement, despite the USA's reluctance to become involved in what it saw as an essentially European affair. Churchill appealed to him for help in March 1941, and Roosevelt persuaded Congress to pass the Lend-Lease Act. This allowed the United States to lend war materials to a country whose defence was seen as necessary for the ultimate safety of the States. The relationship between Britain and the United States was strengthened further when Churchill and Roosevelt met in August 1941. They issued the 'Atlantic Charter', in which they stated their mutual reasons for resisting aggression.

ABOVE: **President Roosevelt signs the Lend-Lease Act into law.**

BELOW: **A great merchant flotilla of British and Allied ships assembles near New York as they prepare to take war materiel to Britain under the Lend-Lease Act.**

LEFT: **An Allied merchant ship is guided through a minefield by means of semaphore.**

Italian defeats

Italian forces had invaded British Somaliland in August 1940. This had initially forced a retreat, but the British had begun to gather a large force of tanks in the area. This meant that when the Italian army staged an invasion of Egypt from Libya in September, the British and Commonwealth forces were able to push them back to Benghazi with comparative speed. Abyssinia, which had been invaded and occupied by Italy in 1935, was also liberated. Mussolini faced a similar disaster in Greece; after invading in October 1940, the Italians met with stiff resistance and were pushed back to Albania by November 1940. To make matters worse, the British attacked the Italian navy at Taranto, its main base, on November 11. Torpedoes were dropped by aircraft and were, for the first time, effective in shallow water – the British lost two planes, but the Italians lost half their fleet.

To reverse Italy's losses, Hitler intervened. His troops had been steadily moving across the Balkans, bringing Romania, Bulgaria and Yugoslavia under his domination. In April 1941 he ordered his Panzers southward to complete the invasion of Greece. He also strengthened the Axis powers in North Africa. By the end of April his Afrika Korps, under the command of General Erwin Rommel, had driven the British out of Libya, back across Egypt and to within range of the Suez Canal.

Sinking of the Bismarck

In May 1941 the German battleship *Bismarck* sailed from the Baltic to the Atlantic on a mission to attack the vital Atlantic convoys, where she could have done great damage. She was undoubtedly the greatest surface threat to their safety. As she passed through the Denmark Strait on May 24 she was intercepted by Britain's great battleship HMS *Hood*. The ships opened fire. The *Hood* received a series of direct hits and sank within minutes with the loss of 1415 men; only three survived. This served to further demonstrate the danger the *Bismarck* represented, and efforts to sink it were redoubled. Once the *Bismarck* was out in the Atlantic she was pursued by British warships and rather elderly torpedo-carrying Swordfish planes. Skirmishing by the Swordfishes disabled the *Bismarck's* steering mechanism leaving her vulnerable. The warships moved in and finished the ship off on May 27.

TOP: **German paratroopers board transport planes in Greece bound for Crete, to where the remainder of the Greek and British armies had retreated.**

ABOVE: **German paratroopers deploy in Crete with minimal equipment, as most of their supplies were dropped separately. This provided a twofold advantage to the Allies, for the Germans were outgunned, and much of their kit was captured.**

ABOVE LEFT: **The Germans had taken control of Crete by the end of May 1941. Many of the Allied troops were evacuated, but about 18,000 were captured.**

BELOW: **South Africans charge through an Italian smokescreen in Libya.**

LEFT: **The Indian army faces the Italians in Eritrea in April 1941.**

PANEL: **Survivors of the *Bismarck* are picked up by the Royal Navy.**

Soviets occupy Baltic States

Following the invasion of Poland and a German-Soviet treaty governing Lithuania, the Soviet Union forced the Baltic countries to allow the stationing of Soviet troops in their territories under pacts of "mutual assistance." Finland rejected the Soviet Union's territorial demands and was invaded by communist forces in November 1939. The resulting conflict ended in March 1940 with Finnish concessions. France and the United Kingdom, treating the Soviet attack on Finland as tantamount to entering the war on the side of the Germans, responded to the Soviet invasion by supporting the USSR's expulsion from the League of Nations. In June 1940, the Soviet Armed Forces invaded and occupied the neutral Baltic States.

JULY 14, 1941
Stalin Toasts British Pact

Britain and Russia yesterday simultaneously announced the signing of a Pact declaring their full determination to defeat Hitler. The terms said:

1. The two Governments mutually undertake to render each other assistance and support of all kinds in the war against Hitlerite Germany;

2. They further undertake that, during this war, they will neither negotiate nor conclude an armistice or treaty except by mutual agreement.

The agreement came into force immediately on its signing in Moscow on Saturday by Sir Stafford Cripps, British Ambassador, and M. Molotov, Soviet Foreign Commissar. After the signing, Stalin joined in the toast to the Pact, drunk in champagne. Poland will be joined to the pact in the course of the next few days.

Negotiations between the Poles and the Russians have so far progressed speedily and satisfactorily. This is due as much to the willingness of the Poles to face the realities of the present situation as to the receptiveness of the Russians and their diplomatic contacts with the British and United States Governments. It would, of course, be paradoxical that the differences between these two neighbouring States, now allied to Britain for the overthrow of Hitler, should be allowed to remain unsettled.

Stalin's act in September 1939 when he occupied half Poland (by agreement with Hitler), will be repudiated. After this has been done, normal diplomatic relations will be restored and arrangements made for the release of the 200,000 Polish war prisoners held by the Russians, for service in the common cause.

OPPOSITE ABOVE RIGHT: **Russian Leader, Josef Stalin, poses for an official photograph.**

OPPOSITE BELOW: **In January 1940 the frozen bodies of Russian soldiers lie along the roadside after the Battle of Suomussalmi in Finland.**

OPPOSITE ABOVE LEFT: **After the Finns recaptured territory from the Russians in the Petsamo region of northern Finland, the bodies of the Russian casualties were collected together ready for burial. The corpses were permanently frozen into the positions in which they died.**

THIS PAGE: **Russian tanks on patrol and in action on the battlefield in July 1941. Soviet armoured forces used a mix of self-propelled light anti-tank guns which could move at great speed whilst firing rapidly, along with much larger tanks equipped with a 6 inch gun set on a revolving turret.**

Pearl Harbor

On Sunday December 7, 1941, the war became a truly global one. Just before eight in the morning, Pearl Harbor, the US naval base in Hawaii, was attacked by almost 200 Japanese fighter planes. The strike came without a declaration of war and caught the navy completely unaware. An hour after the planes had returned to the six aircraft carriers which had escorted them, a second wave of a similar size struck. In total, 19 warships were damaged or destroyed and more than 2,400 people were killed. The scale of the destruction might have been even worse had the US Navy's aircraft carriers not been out on manoeuvres.

Tension between the United States and Japan had been mounting for some years. Japan desired to be the dominant power in East Asia, and the decline of Britain, France and the Netherlands had made this possible. However, the United States, with its presence in the Philippines and interests in the resources of the East Indies, continued to pose a major hurdle. Japan felt squeezed by the United States since Washington had imposed an oil embargo and aided China in the Sino-Japanese War in response to Japan's aggressive expansionism. Attempts to reach a diplomatic solution to their dispute failed as Roosevelt was anxious not to be seen as appeasing Japan in the manner that Hitler had been appeased before the war.

By November 1941, Japan's fuel supplies were running dangerously low and the navy resolved to capture the oilfields of the Dutch East Indies. Fearing that the United States might declare war as a result, and convinced that a war was one day inevitable, Japanese pilots launched a pre-emptive strike on the US fleet.

DAILY MAIL   DECEMBER 8, 1941

Japan declares War on Britain and America

Japan to-night declared war on Britain and the United States after launching full-scale naval and air attacks on two of America's main bases in the Pacific - Pearl Harbour, in Hawaii, and Guam, between Hawaii and the Philippine Islands.

Already the Dutch East Indies have announced themselves at war with Japan, and the formal British and American declarations are expected in a matter of hours.

Quickly recovering from the first attacks, American warships steamed out of Pearl Harbour, and it was later reported that a Japanese aircraft-carrier had been sunk. Four Japanese submarines and six aircraft are also said to have been destroyed.

The Columbia Broadcasting System claims to have picked up a message saying that two British cruisers were sunk by Japanese planes attacking Singapore. This report is completely without confirmation. Another message, equally without support but well within the bounds of possibility, is that Japanese warships have been engaged by British and American naval units in the Western Pacific. This report emanates from the Tokio correspondent of a Japanese newspaper in Shanghai quoting an announcement by Imperial Headquarters.

Early reports that Manila, the American base in the Philippine Islands, had been raided were followed by messages that all is quiet there, apart from aircraft taking off either on reconnaissance or to engage Japanese shipping.

Mr. Stimson, Secretary of War, has ordered the entire United States Army into uniform. This applies to 1,600,000, including thousands of officers and men who are on duty in administrative posts and hitherto have been allowed to wear civilian clothes.

To-night Mr. Roosevelt ordered the Army and Navy to carry out undisclosed orders, already prepared for 'the defence of the United States.'

OPPOSITE ABOVE RIGHT: **Smoke and debris fill the air as the Japanese attack Pearl Harbor.**

OPPOSITE MIDDLE RIGHT: **The USS *Arizona* sinks, engulfed in smoke and flames.**

OPPOSITE BELOW: **Smoke billows from the USS *Shaw* turning the blue Hawaiian sky black.**

TOP: **The Japanese attack on Pearl Harbor disabled the US Pacific allowing Japan to push Into southeast Asia with little opposition.**

ABOVE: **Stunned Americans rushed to enlist in the armed services. Here men enrol for the US Army Air Force (USAAF) under the shadow of Lady Liberty in New York.**

RIGHT: **A line of Japanese battleships with the *Mitsu* nearest the camera.**

BELOW: **The huge propeller and part of the hull of the *Arizona* protrude from the water after the attack.**

America declares war

The day after Pearl Harbor, President Roosevelt delivered a speech to a joint session of Congress saying that December 7, 1941 was a 'date that will live in infamy' and requesting that Congress declare a state of war against Japan. Within hours both houses had voted overwhelmingly in favour of the war. Only one vote was cast against in either chamber, Congresswoman Jeanette Rankin from Montana opposed the war on account of her pacifist beliefs. Britain declared war against Japan on the same day. Three days later, on December 11, Japan's allies, Germany and Italy, declared war on the United States.

RIGHT: **The President signs the declaration of war against Japan, just hours after delivering his speech to Congress.**

BELOW RIGHT: **Roosevelt is flanked by Vice President Henry Wallace, Speaker Samuel Rayburn, and his son, Captain James Roosevelt as he delivers his 'Infamy speech' in the House of Representatives.**

BELOW LEFT: **Factories engaged in war work were asked to put up this poster to inspire their employees.**

BOTTOM: **President Roosevelt addresses a joint session of the US Congress requesting a declaration of war against Japan.**

TO ALL DEFENSE WORKERS . . .

The President of the United States said:

"I APPEAL . . .

"to the owners of plants
"to the managers
"to the workers
"to our own Government employees
"to put every ounce of effort into producing these munitions swiftly and without stint.   And with this appeal I give you the pledge that all of us who are officers of your Government will devote ourselves to the same whole-hearted extent to the great task which lies ahead.

"We must be the great arsenal of democracy.   For us this is an emergency as serious as war itself.   We must apply ourselves to our task with the same resolution, the same sense of urgency, the same spirit of patriotism and sacrifice as we would show were we at war."

★   ★   ★

Let's get squarely behind our President's appeal.

★   ★

Let's work together building that "GREAT ARSENAL OF DEMOCRACY" in record time.

★

Increase PRODUCTION! - That's our No. 1 job!

Let's go!

ABOVE LEFT: Police in Paducah, Kentucky, exchange their patrol cars for pedal bikes in order to conserve rubber, an import from the East Indies, which would inevitably grow scarce.

LEFT: Americans register for sugar ration books, May 1942. Sugar was America's first rationed commodity of the war.

TOP: Japanese men leave a California hotel after being picked up by the FBI.

ABOVE: The camp at Manzanar, California, that housed more than 60,000 Japanese citizens and Japanese Americans during the war.

BELOW: Hundreds of residents of Tillamook, Oregon, meet to discuss civil defence in the event of a Japanese invasion of the West Coast.

DAILY MAIL DECEMBER 9, 1941

Congress declares war on Japan

Marines with fixed bayonets guarded the Capitol to-day as the United States Congress formally declared war on Japan. They voted 25 minutes after President Roosevelt, in a message denouncing Japan's aggression, had called for this action.

Mr. Roosevelt was frequently and loudly cheered during his address. He described yesterday as 'a date that will live in infamy.' The United States, he said, was at peace with Japan, and at her solicitation was still in consultation with her Government's representatives. 'Indeed, one hour after Japanese air squadrons had commenced bombing the American island of Hawaii, the Japanese Ambassador and his colleague delivered to our Secretary of State a formal reply to a recent American message. It contained no threat or hint of war,' he said.

'It will be recorded that the distance of Hawaii from Japan makes it obvious that the attack was deliberately planned many days or even weeks ago. During the intervening time the Japanese Government has deliberately set out to deceive the United States by false statements and expressions of hope for continued peace.

'The attack yesterday on the Hawaiian Islands has caused severe damage to American naval and military forces. I regret to tell you that very many American lives have been lost. In addition, American ships have been reported torpedoed on the high seas between San Francisco and Honolulu. Yesterday the Japanese Government also launched an attack against Malaya.

'Last night, Japanese forces attacked Hongkong. Last night Japanese forces attacked Guam. Last night Japanese forces attacked the Philippine Islands. Last night the Japanese attacked Wake Island. And this morning the Japanese attacked Midway Island.

'As Commander-in-Chief of the Army and Navy, I have directed that all measures be taken for our defence, but always will our whole nation remember the character of the onslaught against us. No matter how long it may take us to overcome this premeditated invasion, the American people in their righteous might will win through to absolute victory.'

American women at war

Women took on many paid jobs in temporary new munitions factories and in old factories that had been converted from civilian products like car manufacturing. This was the 'Rosie the Riveter' phenomenon. 'Rosie the Riveter' became a cultural icon representing the American women who worked in factories that produced munitions and war supplies.

Women also filled many traditionally female jobs that were created by the war boom—as waitresses, for example. And they worked at jobs that previously had been held by men—such as bank teller or shoe salesperson. Nearly one million women worked as so called 'government girls,' taking jobs in the federal government, mainly in Washington, DC, that had previously been held by men or were newly created to deal with the war effort.

Women began to gain more respect and men realized that women actually could work outside the home. They fought for equal pay and made a huge impact on the United States workforce.

ABOVE LEFT: **Women workers, trained for aviation work, are busy on the assembly line of the Glenn L. Martin aircraft plant in Baltimore in February, 1942 where hundreds of bombers are being turned out. They have taken the place of the men called up for the armed forces.**

ABOVE RIGHT: **With New York skyscrapers looming through the clouds of gas, U.S army nurses at Fort Jay, Governors Island, New York, wear gas masks as they drill as part of defense precautions in December, 1941.**

BELOW RIGHT: **Mrs Morton Stern is taking the fingerprint of Mrs Mabel Glenby at the headquarters of the American Women's voluntary services in New York City. In the background are other women who are registering for war work. The**

American Women's Voluntary Service (A.W.V.S) announced that 10,000 women had enrolled for defence training courses in the first week of the war.

BELOW: **Members of the American Women's Voluntary Service being received by the US squadron commanders, Lowell Beatty of New York and Harold Baker of Westchester Unit in Decmber, 1941. The women reported for instruction in coast guard patrol duty at 97th Street and Hudson River.**

US Tanks for the Front Line

Design of the M-3 Tank commenced in July 1940, and the first were fielded in late 1941. The US Army needed a good tank immediately and not a perfect tank later, and coupled with Great Britain's demand for medium tanks immediately, the M-3 was brought into production by late 1940. It was well-armed and -armored for the period, but was withdrawn from front line duty as soon as the M-4 Sherman became available in large numbers.

RIGHT: The last step in the manufacture of the M-3 medium tank was to lift them by crane into flat cars, clamp them down and cover them with tarpaulin. Cars loaded with U.S. tanks, having been thoroughly tested by army officers, would leave Detroit's Chrysler Tank arsenal on a daily basis.

MIDDLE RIGHT: At the start of the war, the Watervliet Arsenal was the only gun manufacturing plant in the US to turn out the famous 16 inch and 14 inch cannons for the army and navy. This is a general view of the shop where the big guns were made showing

them in position in the huge machines where the workmen will turn them into finished products after 12 months of hard work. Under its defence program the government increased its personnel at the arsenal and kept the machines running 24 hours a day.

BELOW RIGHT: This photograph, taken at the Chrysler tank arsenal in April, 1942, shows a medium tank being carried overhead for convenience and quick handling. Fewer rivets were used in the new medium tanks than in the M-3s but for those that remained in the blueprints 125-ton 'cold'

riveting machines such as this would save much time and leave no doubt that the rivets were in to stay.

BELOW: Soon after war was declared the grim reality of the conflict comes to San Francisco as big ramparts of sand bags are hastily constructed in front of one of the telephone company's buildings.

Southeast Asia falls to Japan

The conflict in the Pacific escalated rapidly. On December 10, the British navy suffered an appalling blow when two of its largest battleships, the *Repulse* and the *Prince of Wales*, were sunk by Japanese bombers. Japan made several lightning-fast strikes throughout the area, and by the end of the year the US bases at Guam and Wake Island had been captured. Hong Kong fell on Christmas Day. Japanese forces moved swiftly in an attempt to seize control of southeast Asia following the attack on Pearl Harbor and their run of victories in Malaya, Hong Kong, Thailand and the Philippines. They now launched attacks throughout the Pacific; in January 1942, Manila, the Dutch East Indies, Kuala Lumpur and Burma were invaded.

Burma

This put the Allies under immense pressure. British troops in Malaya were forced to retreat to Singapore by February. The city fell on February 15, and about 80,000 British and Australians were captured. Later in February, Japan attacked Australia itself, bombing the northern city of Darwin. Then the Japanese landed on the island of Java on February 26, defeating British and Dutch naval forces in the Battle of the Java Sea. By early spring, it seemed that the Japanese were almost invincible. British troops had been forced to withdraw across the mainland of Burma towards the Indian border, and the Japanese were continuing to capture islands throughout the western Pacific.

DAILY MAIL DECEMBER 27, 1941
Hong Kong's last stand

The full story of the Battle of Hongkong was issued by the War Office last night.

It starts with December 8, when the Japanese attacked our troops on the mainland and we withdrew into 'Gindrinkers Line,' and ends with Christmas Day when the last of the island garrison was forced to capitulate.

The Hongkong garrison consisted of two British, two Canadian, and two Indian battalions and the Hongkong Volunteer Defence Force. These were: the 2nd Bn. Royal Scots, 1st Bn. Middlesex Regt., a battalion of Winnipeg Grenadiers, a battalion of Royal Rifles of Canada, 2/14th Bn. Punjabis, and 5/7th Bri. Rajputs, with the normal complement of R.A., R.E., R. Sigs. units, and auxiliary services. Units of the Royal Navy and the Hongkong Naval Volunteer Reserve and detachments of Royal Marines co-operated with the military forces.

The geographical features of the colony, states the War Office, its isolation, and the fact that its only aerodrome was on the mainland precluded the possibility of air support.

On the morning of December 8, a Japanese division, with a second division in immediate reserve, crossed the frontier on the mainland. Demolitions were made, and our troops withdrew. There was patrol activity, and a men-carrier patrol ambushed and annihilated a Japanese platoon on Castle Peak road.

On the morning of December 11, strong enemy pressure developed on our left flank, held by the Royal Scots. Two companies were driven off by heavy mortar fire, but the situation was stabilised by using all available reserves. The Royal Scots suffered severe casualties. By midday it was decided to evacuate all the mainland except the Devil's Peak position.

Stonecutters Island was heavily bombarded all day. The island was evacuated during the night of the 11th after demolitions had been made.

The island was sporadically bombarded by artillery and from the air. The civil population was reported to be calm, but their morale considerably shaken. Monetary problems and rice distribution gave cause for serious anxiety.

December 13 was a difficult day.

The enemy sent a delegation to negotiate surrender. The proposal was summarily rejected by the Governor (Sir Mark Young).

On December 16 serial bombing and artillery shelling were increased. One enemy aircraft was brought down into the sea.

On the 17th aerial bombardment was directed against the Peak wireless station and other places. No military damage resulted.

On December 22 the enemy landed further troops on the north-east coast. A counter-attack on the 21st from Stanley towards Ty Tan Tak had failed, although a certain number of the enemy were killed at the cost of about 100 Canadian casualties.

On December 23 some ground on Mount Cameron lost during the night was recaptured by the Royal Marines, but counter-attacks by the force at Stanley towards Stanley Mound failed. However, the Middlesex Regiment successfully repulsed a determined attack at Leighton Hill.

It was impossible to conceal the fact that the situation had become exceedingly grave. The troops, who had been fighting unceasingly for many days, were tired out. The water and food supply was desperate. The reservoirs and depots were in enemy hands.

On December 24 the enemy continued to subject the garrison to heavy fire from dive-bombers and mortars, and by means of incendiary bombs set the countryside all round Mount Cameron on fire.

On December 25 the military and naval commanders informed the Governor that no further effective resistance could be made.

America's first victories in the Pacific

The Battle of the Coral Sea took place from May 4-7, 1942. American aircraft carriers off New Guinea intercepted a Japanese invasion force heading towards Papua and the southern Solomon Islands. This was the first naval battle in which all the fighting was done by the pilots of planes launched from aircraft carriers; it was also the first defeat for the Japanese. There were losses on both sides, but the Japanese fleet was turned back with the loss of an aircraft carrier, making the Coral Sea America's first victory in the war with Japan.

Midway and Guadalcanal

One month later, four more Japanese aircraft carriers were destroyed at the Battle of Midway, severely reducing their capabilities. This heralded a clear change in the Allies' fortunes; they were beginning to gain the advantage in the Pacific in terms of the balance of both air and sea power. Allied attacks were launched in the Solomon Islands, and the first landings took place at Guadalcanal on August 7. At first there was little resistance, but the Japanese troops were very swiftly reinforced and fierce fighting was to rage for the rest of 1942. Naval battles also continued, and the Americans inflicted further heavy damage to the Japanese navy and to a supply convoy off Guadalcanal in November. The island was finally won in February 1943 at a cost of thousands of lives. Within days the Americans moved to assist the Australians in pushing the Japanese out of New Guinea. The Australians had already dealt the Japanese their first defeat of the war at Milne Bay in September 1942, and the addition of the Americans was sufficient to win back control of the island by the end of 1943.

OPPOSITE ABOVE: **A Japanese soldier skirmishes with British troops in Burma.**

OPPOSITE MIDDLE: **A scout group of British, American, Chinese and native Kachin troops wade through a river in the Burmese jungle.**

OPPOSITE BELOW: **One of the US Navy's amphibious trucks brings supplies ashore at New Caledonia in the South Pacific. American troops landed on the Free French island-colony in April 1942.**

ABOVE: **A US bomber attacks a Japanese plane in New Guinea.**

MIDDLE LEFT: **American soldiers manning a howitzer launch an attack in Burma.**

MIDDLE RIGHT: **Men of Britain's 14th Army patrol through swamps in Burma.**

LEFT: **Marines board an LCM landing craft in the Aleutian Islands before setting off to push the Japanese off Kiska Island.**

BELOW: **US troops fire on Japanese positions on the Aleutian island of Attu. The Japanese navy attacked the Aleutians to try to divert the Americans from Midway.**

The Americans arrive in Britain

Meeting in Washington in December 1941, Churchill and Roosevelt agreed that the Allies should concentrate on winning the war in Europe before turning their attentions fully towards the Pacific theatre. This 'Germany First' policy had its critics, but it was agreed that the US and Britain would be stronger fighting together, and that logistically Britain had to confront the Nazi threat first. Nevertheless, the US would keep piling the pressure on Japan and won some key battles at Coral Sea and Midway during 1942.

American troops had begun landing in Britain within weeks of the attack on Pearl Harbor and Hitler's subsequent declaration of war on the US; throughout 1942 they were to arrive in vast numbers. These were the GIs (their equipment was stamped 'General Issue'; hence the name) and they were widely welcomed in Britain.

The GIs proved especially popular with children – they were widely seen as purveyors of treats that had become impossible to find, such as chocolate and sweets. They were also very popular with some British women, some 20,000 of whom would become 'GI brides' by the end of the war. As a result of this, many British men would complain that the Americans were 'oversexed, overpaid and over here'.

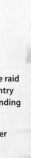

RIGHT: **Just seven weeks after the raid on Pearl Harbor and America's entry into the war, US troops began landing in Britain.**

ABOVE RIGHT: **An American soldier enjoys a Bank Holiday fair in Hampstead.**

MIDDLE RIGHT: **American marines land in Iceland on their way to Britain.**

ABOVE: **A US Jeep makes for an unusual sight amongst the London traffic.**

FAR LEFT: **General Eisenhower watches Charlton Athletic take on Chelsea in the Southern Cup Final at Wembley Stadium.**

FAR LEFT MIDDLE: **Britain was awash with Allied troops. Here Winston Churchill visits Czechoslovak troops with the Czechoslovak President Eduard Benes.**

FAR LEFT BELOW: **American tank crews on manoeuvres in England.**

LEFT: **Eleanor Roosevelt tours through buildings destroyed in the Blitz in London in October 1942.**

BELOW LEFT: **Many women were thrilled that the arrival of the GIs meant that luxury items such as stockings became easier to obtain. Until then many women had painted their legs to give the impression of a seam.**

BOTTOM: **British and American troops arrive in port in advance of the Allied invasion of North Africa, November 1942.**

Stalingrad

Russia's Red Army had managed to hold out over the winter of 1941 and even had some success in pushing the Germans back from Moscow in January. By late spring, however, the German Army had regrouped and a new campaign was planned. This time the intention was to strike towards the Crimea in the south, which would ultimately enable the Germans to take control of the Caucasus where there were significant oil reserves.

In June and July the Germans captured Rostov and Sevastopol, but this initial success was not to last. The German army turned north in August, heading for the important city of Stalingrad, and their advance was slowed by Russian resistance. It finally ground to a halt in the suburbs of Stalingrad itself, and the Germans had to settle in for a long siege instead of a swift advance. Stalingrad was desperately defended, with every patch of ground contested bitterly, and then the Russians launched a counter-offensive as the winter of 1942 began. They inflicted heavy casualties on their enemies and eventually surrounded the Germans to both the north and south of the city. Trapped between the relieving troops and the city's desperate defenders, the German Sixth Army and the Fourth Panzer Division awaited help from a relieving army, as well as urgent supplies of all kinds.

ABOVE: **Russian marines engage the Germans on the Black Sea coast, July 1942.**

TOP RIGHT: **New Red Navy torpedo boats set out on a mission in the Black Sea.**

MIDDLE RIGHT: **A family crouch over the body of their father, murdered during a massacre in the town of Kerch. The bandaged man on the left of the picture was wounded in the head during the massacre and lay still covered with earth and corpses until the Nazis departed.**

RIGHT: **The scene of Nazi terror against the civilian population of Russia in Rostov-on-Don.**

BELOW: **The ruins of Stalingrad's Factory District, where much of the fighting took place.**

Russian victory

It was astonishingly cold – the temperature reached 24 degrees below freezing – and the Germans lacked winter uniforms, food and medicine. Ammunition was also running low, but Hitler refused to allow their surrender – nor could he manage to supply them, effectively condemning the army to a form of mass suicide. By December there was no longer much doubt about the ultimate result, and January 31 saw a massive defeat for the Germans southwest of Stalingrad. On February 2, 1943 the German commander, Von Paulus, finally surrendered, disobeying Hitler. The Russians took over 90,000 prisoners, amongst whom were twenty-four generals; many more, on both sides, had died. This was the German army's greatest-ever defeat and a major turning point on the Eastern Front. The Russians now began to push the Germans back to the west.

TOP: Soldiers raise the Red Flag above a building in a recaptured part of Stalingrad.

ABOVE: Stalingrad residents welcome reinforcements from the Red Army.

BELOW: Many Soviet civilians were trapped in the city and had to make their homes amongst the rubble, in basements, or even in shell holes.

LEFT: Once the Germans had been defeated, these women were free to emerge from the basement which had been their home for the duration of the battle.

DAILY MAIL FEBRUARY 1, 1943

Stalingrad army wiped out

Field-Marshal Paulus, Commander-in-Chief of the German Sixth Army and Fourth Tank Army at Stalingrad, was captured by the Russians yesterday a few hours after he had been promoted to the highest rank by special proclamation from Hitler's headquarters.

He was seized with his staff when Soviet troops stormed the Ogpu headquarters in the heart of the city and completed the greatest disaster that has befallen Germany in this war.

It is now revealed as a disaster of unsuspected proportions. Instead of 220,000 men, the trapped army consisted of 330,000 troops, it was announced by Moscow in a special communique last night.

In addition to the Sixth Army, the Fourth Panzer Army has been trapped and destroyed. Thirteen German and two Rumanian generals and 46,000 troops have been captured. Five thousand were taken prisoner with Marshal Paulus yesterday.

Booty taken between January 10 and 30 includes 744 aircraft, 1,517 tanks, and 6,523 guns.

Resistance and collaboration

During the Second World War the Nazis controlled a vast swath of Europe from France to the Soviet Union. Throughout their occupied territories and vassal states the Germans found people prepared to work with them and people intent upon working against them. Those who collaborated usually did so because they were sympathetic to Nazi ideology or were pragmatists willing to work with whoever was in charge. They assisted the Germans by forming puppet governments, deporting Jews and arresting members of the resistance; some even joined voluntary units of the dreaded Waffen SS. Those opposed to German occupation or to Nazi ideology joined organized resistance movements or engaged in individual acts of defiance. Their activities ranged from hiding Jews and sabotaging communications to killing collaborators and providing intelligence to the Allies. Many others did not actively participate in resistance or collaboration and simply tried to survive the occupation – these people have sometimes been criticized as passive collaborators.

The reaction to the German occupation was not uniform across Europe; there was inevitably more resistance activity wherever the German presence was stronger and German rule more direct. Different national groups also responded to the German presence in different ways and some nations even welcomed the Germans as liberators from other oppressors – such was the case in Croatia and Estonia where the Germans were regarded as liberators from Serb and Russian domination respectively.

Français ! souvenez-vous
ici habite un
COLLABORATEUR

Ce papillon ne peut être apposé sur la porte d'un COLLABORATEUR qu'après enquête et autorisation des Services du Contre Espionnage.

Uprisings in Warsaw

From November 1939 Warsaw's Jewish population was forced to move into a ghetto, which was sealed-off from the rest of the city the following year. Jews from all over Poland and Europe were sent to live in the Warsaw Ghetto where thousands died from starvation and disease. From July 1942 the Nazis began a major purge of the Ghetto and hundreds of thousands of people were sent to their deaths at Treblinka. In early 1943, after news of the exterminations had reached the Ghetto, the remaining population rose up in rebellion. Using weapons that had been smuggled in or improvised, the rebels held out against the German army for almost a month. Thousands were killed during the uprising and the survivors were deported to death camps or executed on the spot.

The following year the Polish Home Army, the main Polish resistance movement, rose up in rebellion hoping to liberate Warsaw before the fast-approaching Soviet troops arrived. The uprising began on August 1, 1944 and the 50,000 strong Polish Home Army met with some early successes. However, the Germans soon sent in reinforcements and the Luftwaffe began a relentless bombardment of the city. The rebels were slowly worn down and no relief came from Soviet forces, which had stopped just short of the city – ostensibly on the orders of Stalin who did not want the Polish Home Army to take over. With more than 200,000 dead and much of the city destroyed, the rebels surrendered on October 2, 1944. The Russians seized the city three months later.

OPPOSITE MIDDLE LEFT: **Marshal Pétain inspects French troops at Châteauroux, in unoccupied France.** Pétain ruled Vichy France in collaboration with the Nazis in order to spare southern France from direct German rule. The Vichy government actively supported Nazi racial policies against the Jews, and thousands were rounded up, placed in concentration camps, and later transported to death camps in the east.

OPPOSITE TOP LEFT: **Vidkun Quisling awaits his trial in Oslo at the end of the war.** The name of the wartime Premier of Norway, who was appointed upon the orders of Hitler, has become synonymous with collaboration.

OPPOSITE TOP RIGHT: **Quisling gives the Nazi salute as he inspects German troops in Norway.**

OPPOSITE MIDDLE RIGHT: **The Allies drop supplies to the Resistance in Nazi occupied Belgium.**

OPPOSITE MIDDLE: **'Here lives a collaborator'.** Anyone suspected by the Resistance of collaborating with the Germans might have woken to find this sign posted on their front door during the night.

OPPOSITE BELOW: **French Resistance fighters are drilled on the edge of a field close to the treeline so they can duck for cover.**

ABOVE: **In hunger and dispair, members of the Polish resistance await the arrival of the Nazis following their surrender.**

FAR LEFT: **This still from a film smuggled out of France reveals daily life in the French resistance.** When possible, the day began with the raising of the Tricolour.

LEFT ABOVE: **Resistance fighters practise shooting in the foothills of the French Alps.**

LEFT: **Italian Resistance fighters launch an attack against Fascists in a Milan street.**

BELOW: **The ruins of Warsaw following the failed uprising in August 1944.**

El Alamein

The start of 1942 saw something of a stand-off in North Africa; both sides were regrouping on either side of the Gazala Line. Rommel launched his next attack on the British in May, as the Germans were attacking in Russia. His army outflanked the British and forced them to make a rapid withdrawal to Tobruk – which was lost by June. Following that, the British Eighth Army retreated eastwards to El Alamein. Here it was possible for them to be reinforced, both swiftly and to a considerable extent, from the Suez Canal. There were sustained German attacks during July and August, but the British were able to hold the defensive Alamein Line. They were ready to strike back by October, under the inspirational command of General Montgomery, who was sent to lead the Eighth Army in August. During the night of October 23 an enormous artillery bombardment began, followed by a frontal assault against Rommel's forces. Progress was steady though slow initially, but the advance picked up speed and Rommel began to retreat on November 3. The Germans were then quickly pushed back into Libya.

ABOVE RIGHT: **An American-built Maryland bomber of the South African Air Force strikes a German supply convoy in the Libyan desert.**

ABOVE: **Part of the vast Allied armada heading to the North African coast during Operation Torch.**

MIDDLE RIGHT: **Troops bring stores ashore on the North African coast during the Torch landings.**

RIGHT: **Wading through the Mediterranean Sea, American troops come ashore in Algeria.**

BELOW: **Headed by a standard bearer, US troops march towards an airfield near Algiers on the first day of Operation Torch.**

Operation Torch

Five days later, on November 8, a large-scale invasion of French North Africa was launched under the command of US General Dwight Eisenhower. It was known as Operation Torch, and had the honour of being the largest seaborne expedition in history until it was dwarfed by the Normandy landings.

Stalin had been demanding that the Allies open a second front in Europe to relieve some of the pressure on the Red Army, which was defending an enormous front. Roosevelt agreed with the strategy in principle, but was advised against it by his generals. Churchill was also sceptical; he had authorized 'a reconnaissance in force to test the enemy defences' at the French port at Dieppe in August 1942. It was a disaster. The force was withdrawn after only nine hours, by which time thousands of troops — mostly Canadians — had been either killed or captured. Instead, Churchill advocated opening a new front in North Africa. By capturing Tunisia, the Allies would severely disrupt the enemy's supply lines and could engage them on two fronts.

TOP: Medium bombers of the U.S. Army Air Force in the Middle East are seen flying in formation over the desert in late October 1942. The planes are camouflaged so that they blend into the background colour. These are the planes that are harassing the supply lines and bases of the Axis in North Africa.

ABOVE: American troops wade ashore at Arzeu, having been delivered from their ships by landing craft.

RIGHT: General Eisenhower and General Giraud inspect a Guard of Honour of French troops during a victory parade in Tunis, Tunisia in May 1943.

BELOW: The Torch landings, commanded by General Eisenhower, began on November 8 with troops deployed at Safi and Casablanca in Morocco, and on beaches at Algiers and Oran in Algeria. After brief conflicts with French forces Admiral Darlan, commander of Vichy France, ordered a ceasefire on November 11, and French cooperation was assured. The Allies now began to close in on the Axis armies from both sides, forcing them into Tunisia.

Pushing Germany out of Africa

There was little resistance to the Allied landings, and Admiral Darlan, the commander of Vichy France, whose forces were occupying the area, ordered a ceasefire just two days later. He also appealed to the French navy to leave Toulon, where they were based, and join the Allies. Hitler immediately scrapped Marshal Pétain's collaborationist Vichy government and ordered the full occupation of France, which took place on November 11. The French immediately scuttled their fleet to deny the Germans additional naval power.

By the end of January 1943 Montgomery's army had pushed the Germans back westward from Egypt through Libya and General Eisenhower was pushing east. Trapped between the two, the position of the Axis forces was hopeless. Rommel himself left for Europe, handing over to General von Arnim. The Axis army – about 250,000 men – surrendered to the Allies in May.

RIGHT: **Old Glory, the American Flag, flies above the ruins of a North African town.**

BELOW: **The liberated French population of Algiers give the V-for-Victory sign as American troops march through the town.**

ABOVE: The first operational task of the United States Army in the European theatre of operations, the occupation of French North Africa was begun on November 8 by U.S. Rangers simultaneously landed at strategic points. Here, an American officer is in conversation with villagers at a point near Oran where a landing was made without opposition.

ABOVE LEFT: America's General Eisenhower (left) with Britain's General Montgomery (right). After pushing the Germans out of Africa, the two men would lead the Allies to victory in Western Europe.

LEFT: Italian soldiers are driven through the streets of Algiers on their way to internment camps.

American troops were charged with maintaining order as locals poured onto the streets to jeer at the POWs.

BELOW: Captured Italians are driven through Algiers to internment camps shortly after the Torch landings.

The home front in Britain

In Britain, women had begun to be conscripted into war work or the forces in December 1941. By 1943, 90 per cent of single women were either serving in the forces themselves or working in war industries – such as munitions and armaments factories and shipyards – replacing the men who were now in the armed forces. They also worked in agriculture, where there were eventually some 80,000 'land girls' in the Women's Land Army.

Life in Britain during the war was often difficult as bombing raids continued and most things were in short supply. Everything from clothes to food and from soap to petrol was rationed and people were encouraged to 'make do and mend', by repairing and reusing everyday items.

With everybody devoting their lives to fighting for their country in some way, there was widespread agreement that post-war British society would have to change to benefit the majority of the population. The way forward was set out in the Beveridge Report, which became an unlikely bestseller. In it, Sir William Beveridge proposed that a system of social security for everyone should be set up after the war, with a National Health Service and a system of family allowances.

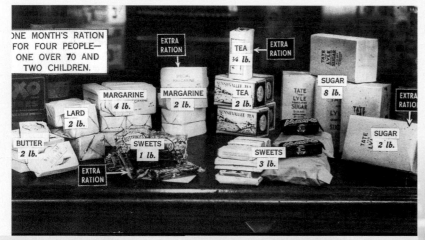

LEFT: German attacks on merchant shipping would bring Britain dangerously close to running out of essential supplies. Bacon, butter and sugar were the first products to be rationed, quickly followed by other foodstuffs and household goods.

BELOW LEFT: Three women of the Women's Land Army ploughing reclaimed land on a farm in Bedford, with the aid of three tractors working in echelon.

ABOVE: Land girls reap the corn harvest on a Buckinghamshire farm.

BELOW: German bombing resulted in temporary evacuations and diversions, further disrupting daily life in Britain.

Easing of restrictions

By 1943, the Allies had superiority in the air, but smaller-scale bombing raids did still occur, particularly over London, and usually in response to attacks on German cities. Perhaps the most tragic incident happened on the night of March 3 during a minor raid in the East End of London; it was not directly attributable to the enemy, however. People were hurrying to enter Bethnal Green Underground station and take shelter, when somebody lost their footing at the top of the stairs and fell. Pressure from behind meant that those in front could not stop, and the resulting crush caused the deaths of 178 people.

The end of the Blitz had brought some small relaxation in regulations, though rationing still continued. Early in 1943 it was ruled that lights in railway carriages could be left on when trains were standing at stations (they had previously been extinguished so that the trains – and thus stations – could not be easily detected from the air), and it was later agreed that traffic lights could be used; pedestrians were allowed to carry undimmed torches.

TOP LEFT: **Making a phone call between protective sandbags in London.**

LEFT: **British people were encouraged to 'Dig for Victory' by growing vegetables wherever there was space. Even bombsites were converted into allotments.**

TOP RIGHT: **Schoolboys take tea in the garden of their damaged home following a raid.**

ABOVE LEFT: **Clothes rationing began in Britain on June 1, 1941. Owing to a shortage of material, people were encouraged to 'make do and mend' by repairing older garments.**

ABOVE RIGHT: **Despite being bombed out of their office building, work continues in the street.**

The Baedeker Raids: Britain Blitzed again

The Baedeker Raids took place from April 1942 to the end of June. The name came from Baedeker travel guides of Britain as the press reported that this was how the targets were selected. Instead of attacking the industrial towns and cities, suddenly all the picturesque tourist cities such as Bath, Norwich, Exeter, Canterbury and York became targets. They did not have the air defences of the larger cities and consequently 1,637 were killed with 1,760 injured. Over 50,000 homes were lost. It was believed that these raids were in response to the Allied bombing of Lübeck in northern Germany. It had been targeted as a base used to supply German troops on the Russian front.

ABOVE: **The ruins of St Andrew's Church in Bath, gutted by fire after a Baedeker raid in April 1942.**

RIGHT: **York's 15th- century Guildhall in flames, after a raid in retribution for RAF attacks on Baltic ports.**

BELOW: **Searching for victims in the ruins of St John's Roman Catholic Church which received a direct hit. One of the priests was killed.**

ABOVE LEFT: A comic moment as Pioneer Corps come across a relic from the past in the rubble of bombed Bath.

ABOVE: During a raid on the city of Cambridge in August 1942, the University Union Society's building suffered the effects of blast damage.

LEFT: Bomb damage to one of Bath's beautiful Georgian Crescents.

BELOW: Thick grey dust covered the houses and roadway after the havoc caused in a Bath thoroughfare by Nazi raiders.

Working conditions

Even though women in Britain daily proved their abilities as part of the workforce, they were paid considerably less than their male counterparts. The average woman's pay in 1943 was £3 2s 11d, just over 50 per cent of the £6 1s 4d that was the average male pay. Additionally, working conditions were often very basic. As munitions factories had generally been converted from peacetime production – not necessarily of munitions – or were hastily converted or constructed buildings, and as many of the machine tools were used for jobs for which they were not initially intended, safety was frequently a serious concern. Many factories were designed for men and far fewer workers than employed during the war, so that facilities like toilets and rest rooms were in short supply. Normal working hours were long and when there were calls for increased production, such as after the retreat from Dunkirk, the working day could be extended, so that women found themselves working from 8 a.m. to 7 p.m.

ABOVE LEFT: **Women in the "Pick and Shovel Brigade".** At a new aerodrome somewhere in East Anglia about 100 women and girls are doing navvies' work with zest and enjoyment. Here they are laying pipes for drainage each side of the runway.

MIDDLE LEFT: **These women,** filling sandbags, were the first to be employed to clear air-raid debris and help make buildings safe.

LEFT: **Mrs Eilen Glassett,** drilling wing spars for a Halifax bomber, had been a sales assistant in a womenswear shop in London's West End. Like many women she gave up her peacetime job to go into the factories.

ABOVE: **Miss Louisa Lines, aged 20,** formerly a Yorkshire cotton machinist, painting along the scuppers of a nearly finished merchant ship. Women helped in the high speed ship production in British shipyards. Women were fast taking their places with the men in the yards, painting, plate marking, and generally carrying out tasks which, before the war, were considered hard even for the men.

TOP LEFT: **Mrs Flannigan, a woman bricklayer, works to repair bomb damage to a Southern Railway arch in London.**

ABOVE RIGHT: **A woman works on making a shell casing at a factory in Southern England.**

ABOVE: **In January 1941, Britain's first dustwomen assumed their roles in Ilford. The council employed 'eight comely dustbin-emptiers'.**

RIGHT: **'She-navvies' cheerfully wheel barrow loads of heavy stones at a railway goods yard. '**

Bombing Germany

For the first two years of the war, Britain did not launch a comprehensive air offensive against Germany's cities. There was strategic bombing of military and industrial targets within Germany, but it was not until 1942 that Britain began indiscriminately raiding Germany with the intention of breaking civilian morale. Arthur 'Bomber' Harris took charge of Bomber Command in February 1942 and began planning for the aerial bombing of German cities. The test case for the new tactic was the historic city of Lubeck in northern Germany, which was struck on the night of March 28, 1942. The town's old buildings were easily set alight by the incendiary bombs dropped by the RAF, causing widespread destruction and loss of life.

1,000-Bomber Raids

Two months after Lubeck, Harris assembled his bombers for a strike against Cologne, an industrial city on the Rhine. Operation Millennium, as it was codenamed, employed 1,047 aircraft, making it the largest fleet yet seen in aerial warfare. The raid was originally intended for Hamburg, Germany's second-largest city and a major site of U-boat production, but it was switched to Cologne because of poor weather. On the night of May 30, the aircraft flew in a tight stream, maintaining height and speed, both to avoid collisions and to limit German radar detection. The mission was achieved more quickly than had ever been attempted, even for a much smaller force. Although some of the crews missed their intended target, almost 900 planes bombed Cologne, releasing 1,455 tons of bombs, two thirds of which were incendiary devices.

ABOVE RIGHT: **Members of the German Safety Service tackle a blaze caused by incendiary bombs.**

FAR RIGHT: **An American Liberator bomber plunges towards the ground after being damaged by anti-aircraft fire.**

RIGHT: **Low-flying RAF bombers strike a power station in Cologne.**

BELOW: **Berliners clear away debris following an air raid.**

Hamburg and Dresden

The RAF proceeded to relentlessly bomb Germany by night, and from 1943, they were joined by the American Air Force (USAAF) which bombed by day. This relentless round the clock bombardment never directly achieved its aim of forcing Germany into submission by breaking civilian morale, but it did play a vital role in wearing Germany down in preparation for the overland invasion.

In late July 1943, the RAF and the USAAF launched Operation Gomorrah, a series of devastating raids on Hamburg. Almost 3,000 sorties were flown over the city leading to the deaths of an estimated 40,000 people, most of whom perished in a great firestorm that engulfed the city on the night of July 27. A firestorm caused by a heavy raid on Dresden killed a similar number of people in February 1945. Dresden was singled out for the raid because it was an important transport hub and was being used to send troops and supplies to the Eastern Front. The death toll was higher than might have been expected because Dresden's population had swelled in number as a result of the thousands of refugees who had poured into the city in the empty trains returning from the front.

LEFT: US airmen report back to an officer following a successful raid on industrial sites near Berlin. The markings on the back of this navigator's jacket indicate the number of missions he has completed.

BELOW LEFT: A Swastika is draped over a bombed-out building to commemorate Hitler's 55th birthday in April 1944. Despite the relentless bombing campaign, there was no revolution against the Nazi regime. Some continued to support Hitler, others feared his terror network or Soviet reprisals; the rest became stoically resigned to their fate.

BELOW: Factories and an airfield in Berlin burn after heavy bombing. Initially, Berlin was spared the worst of the aerial onslaught because it was too far away for the RAF to mount a sustained campaign. However, improved technology and the arrival of the Americans changed that and Berlin was bombed severely from November 1943 until the last months of the war.

TOP: **The Mohne Dam is successfully breached by a bouncing bomb during the 'Dambuster' raids of May 1943.**

ABOVE LEFT: **A B17 Flying Fortress crew study their new remote-controlled chin-turret which provided better protection against frontal fighter assaults.**

ABOVE RIGHT: **Despite massive damage to the tail of this B17, the pilot managed to return from his bombing mission over Germany and land safely back in Britain.**

Allied offensives in the Pacific, 1943–44

Midway proved to be the last great naval battle for two years. The United States used the ensuing period to turn its vast industrial potential into actual ships, planes, and trained aircrew. At the same time, Japan, lacking an adequate industrial base or technological strategy, a good aircrew training program, or adequate naval resources and commerce defense, fell further and further behind. In strategic terms the Allies began a long movement across the Pacific, seizing one island base after another. Not every Japanese stronghold had to be captured; some, like Truk, Rabaul, and Formosa, were neutralized by air attack and bypassed. The goal was to get close to Japan itself, then launch massive strategic air attacks, improve the submarine blockade, and finally (only if necessary) execute an invasion.

In November 1943 US Marines sustained high casualties when they overwhelmed the 4,500-strong garrison at Tarawa. This helped the Allies to improve the techniques of amphibious landings, learning from their mistakes and implementing changes such as thorough pre-emptive bombings and bombardment, more careful planning regarding tides and landing craft schedules, and better overall coordination.

The US Navy did not seek out the Japanese fleet for a decisive battle, as Mahanian doctrine would suggest (and as Japan hoped); the Allied advance could only be stopped by a Japanese naval attack, which oil shortages (induced by submarine attack) made impossible.

BELOW: **US Air Mastery on Guadalcanal. 'Wildcat' fighter planes lined up and ready for US Navy and Marine pilots at an airfield on Guadalcanal Island. Although US Marines had withdrawn from the Island, the Marine Air Force was still there fighting hard with Army and Navy pilots. Up until February the Japanese had lost 876 planes – five times that of the American losses.**

Burma 1943

The Japanese invasion of Burma in 1942 had successfully cut off supply routes to China along the Burma Road and placed Japanese troops dangerously close to the Indian border. Japanese commanders had hoped that Indian forces in the area would revolt against the British. However, although some captured soldiers were formed into an army to fight against the Allies, colonial Indian divisions, which had fought alongside British troops in North Africa, were redeployed to Burma in 1943 where they fought with great distinction. Now under the overall command of Lord Mountbatten, British troops were reinforced and received greater air support, enabling them to maintain defensive positions deep in the Burmese jungles; the employment of guerrilla tactics would result in some successful campaigns against the Japanese. Major General Orde Wingate formed and led the 77th Indian Infantry Brigade, otherwise known as the Chindits, which adopted the tactic of 'Long Range Penetration', operating in columns deep inside enemy territory, sabotaging infrastructure and ambushing Japanese troops. Although they were eventually ordered to withdraw as air-drops became more difficult, the Chindits had proven that damage could be inflicted on the Japanese in difficult jungle territory.

BELOW: General Frank Merrill and some of his staff discuss new methods to hamper the Japanese headquarters somewhere in the Burmese jungle.

RIGHT: American soldiers waving a greeting from one of the convoy ships arriving at an Australian port, with thousands of U.S. troops and war materials in June 1942.

ABOVE: Native stretcher bearers in New Guinea rest themselves and their casualties in the shade of a coconut grove en route from the front lines near Buna to hospitals in the rear. In skirmishes and large engagements, United States troops killed over a thousand Japanese in five days.

The liberation of Italy

The Allied victory in North Africa in May 1943 altered the state of play in the Mediterranean, making an attack on Italy possible. Italy was in bad shape: the country had lost an estimated 200,000 soldiers in North Africa, more than 200,000 were fighting on the Eastern Front, and about 500,000 were deployed in the Balkans. So when American, British and Canadian troops invaded Sicily in July 1943, the island fell within just six weeks. This rapid defeat in Sicily, combined with the devastating bombing of the mainland, led to the overthrow of Mussolini by the Fascist Grand Council; he was arrested and sent to prison.

In September, the Allies had crossed to the mainland and the new Italian government surrendered. However, this did not bring peace as the Germans in the country continued to resist the Allied advance. Italy was now treated as another of Germany's vassals: Jews were rounded up and deported to Auschwitz, partisans were executed and the country was plundered of its historic artworks. German glider pilots even rescued Mussolini from his remote mountain prison and made him leader of their new puppet state, the 'Italian Social Republic'.

LEFT: Italian soldiers in Sicily surrender.

LEFT MIDDLE: Anzio lies in ruins in the aftermath of Allied raids in preparation for the landings in January 1944.

LEFT BELOW: First news of Italy's surrender reaches London. However, the fighting would get much worse once the Germans took over.

MIDDLE: Roman women gives a rapturous welcome to Allied troops.

FAR LEFT: The people of Naples greet the Allies after having seen off the Germans themselves.

BOTTOM LEFT: A church in Turin damaged during Allied air raids on the major industrial centres in northern Italy on August 8, 1943.

BOTTOM RIGHT: As food grows scarce, the grounds of Milan Cathedral are turned into a cornfield.

The fall of Rome

After encountering some initial difficulties at Salerno, the Allies raced through southern Italy in September 1943. They reached Naples at the end of the month to discover the population of the city had already risen up and pushed the Germans out. The lightning advance ground to a halt in November after the Germans retreated to the 'Gustav Line', a highly defendable position running across the country from the Tyrrhenian to the Adriatic Seas.

Attempts to break the Line during the winter proved costly to the Allies, so a surprise landing was made north of the Gustav Line, at Anzio, on January 22, 1944. In February the Germans counter-attacked in this area and the Allied advance came to a halt. To relieve the pressure on their men at Anzio, the Allies launched an invasion across the Gustav Line at Monte Cassino, the site of an ancient Benedictine abbey. The town did not fall until three months later, and only after the town and abbey had been completely reduced to rubble with great loss of life. With the Gustav Line breached, the Allies linked up with their comrades at Anzio and marched on Rome, liberating the city on June 4, 1944.

Mussolini executed

The Germans continued to resist in Italy for almost a year, and it was not until April 29, 1945 that they finally surrendered. The day before, Mussolini and his mistress had been captured and executed by Italian partisans. Their bodies, along with fifteen others, were hung upside-down from the girders of a petrol station in Milan.

ABOVE LEFT: Monghidoro, just south of Bologna, is liberated by the Allies in October 1944.

MIDDLE LEFT: British troops kick down the door of SS Headquarters in Florence.

BELOW LEFT: Italian partisans search for German stragglers in the town of Cesena following its liberation.

BOTTOM: Seventeen merchant ships in the liberated Italian port of Bari are bombed in a surprise German raid in December 1943.

DAILY MAIL   FEBRUARY 16 1944

Cassino Abbey bombed to a ruin

Front-Line troops of the Fifth Army watched in awed silence to-day the destruction by bomb and shell of Cassino Abbey. They looked on at the terrible bombardment with memories of comrades who had fallen under the guns of the Germans entrenched behind the abbey walls.

It had to be done - this razing of one of the great monuments of the Western World. And it has been done thoroughly after repeated warnings and with all due consideration for civilian life.

Seven waves of Fortresses, Mitchells, and Marauders have reduced the monastery to ruins. When I turned away from the scene an hour ago, the great, grey oblong monastery was nothing but a jagged silhouette against the pale blue sky. The German guns mounted in the abbey have been silenced. No longer is it the strong fortress dominating Cassino and denying us access along 'Highway Six' to Rome.

Doubtless there will be argument for many years to come about the deed that was done between 9 a.m. and 2 p.m., but I don't believe there was one man on our side of the Rapido Valley to-day who felt any regret or remorse, or, indeed, any other emotion save acute interest.

The attack was directed not only against the monastery but against the system of pillboxes and strong-points on the slopes below it.

TOP: American artillery pounds Monte Cassino in February 1944. The abbey was initially spared, but the Allies began shelling it to deny the Germans a key observation post on the Gustav Line.

ABOVE: Monte Cassino Abbey lies in ruins after the battle.

LEFT: Not a building is left undamaged during the Allied offensive on Monte Cassino.

1944: Japan in retreat

The hard-won success of Guadalcanal led to a determined advance, codename Operation Cartwheel, by Allied forces through the Solomon Islands and New Guinea during 1943. Japanese forces had a major HQ in the town of Rabaul on the island of New Britain, garrisoned by around 100,000 troops, and this now became a strategic goal for the Allies in the Pacific Campaign. In the Battle of Tarawa, a heavily fortified atoll that held the key to the recapture of the Marianas, the Allied beach landings in November were met by the first heavy Japanese resistance at the beachhead to date; this would provide useful experience for future Allied landings such as Iwo Jima – but with a high cost in casualties. In the game of chess played out in the Pacific Islands, the steady pushing of the Allied forces could only have one conclusion but the delaying tactics of the totally committed Japanese Imperial Army made progress slow and the loss of life very high – on both sides. But the first months of 1944 proved the tide had turned on Japan.

ABOVE: **Marines on the littered beach at Tarawa covered their ammunition and other gear with camouflaged shelter-halfs in case the Japanese tried an air attack.**

ABOVE RIGHT: **A sub-machine gun in one hand and a grenade in the other, a soldier marches at the head of his men in pursuit of Japanese defenders of New Britain Island in the Southwest Pacific. US troops, in a two-pronged drive, advanced to new positions on the north and south** coasts of New Britain and by March 27, 1944 were less than 170 miles away from the major Japanese base at Rabaul.

BELOW RIGHT: **US Marines attack a Japanese strongpoint during the landing at Tarawa, where some of the 'bloodiest fighting of the campaign took place' to establish an Allied bridgehead on this central Pacific base. Two Marines – barely visible in their camouflaged cloaks – can be seen crouching behind the** shattered stumps of palm trees, having tossed dynamite sticks seen exploding on the Japanese strongpoint.

BELOW: **Marines advance across desolate Darry Island in the wake of fleeing Japanese, as the Marines took Eniwetok Atoll in the Marshall Islands. The palm trees were either uprooted or defoliated by the bombardment before the leathernecks came ashore to clean out the holed-up Japanese in February 1944.**

ABOVE LEFT: **US Marines plunge through the surf at Cape Gloucester, New Britain, after disembarking from a landing craft to push a jeep to shore. An amphibious vehicle nears the beach during landing preparations on the Southwest Pacific island on December 26. Some Marines carry stretchers so that the wounded can be removed to medical stations promptly. US landing forces captured the twin air strips on Cape Gloucester in the initial attacks and then pressed on inland in their campaign against the Japanese.**

ABOVE RIGHT: **American Marines wading ashore at Cape Gloucester, New Britain, had rough surf as well as the enemy to contend with. But they beat both. Other troops can be seen on the beach.**

MIDDLE RIGHT: **A Japanese soldier, cornered by US Marines on Namur Island, holds out his arms in surrender while another Japanese digs his way out of a blasted blockhouse where twenty Japanese were trapped. An enemy soldier lies dead at the foot of the wrecked stairway (centre). Namur was the northern part of Kwajalein Atoll and one of the Japanese island fortresses in the Central Pacific taken by US forces leading up to the seizure of Kwajalein in the Marshall Islands, February 1944.**

MIDDLE LEFT: **American assault troops splash across a shallow stream, near Aitape, where they formed small patrol groups to seek out Japanese defenders of the coastal base on Northern Guinea. US amphibious forces stormed ashore at Aitape and at two points flanking Hollandia, to the west, on April 22, 1944,**

gaining control of an additional 150 mile stretch of the Northern New Guinea coast for the Allies. Supplementary landings six days later aided in blocking escape routes for an estimated 60,000 Japanese troops entrapped in that area of the Southwest Pacific island.

LEFT: **US amphibious tanks line a beach, bringing in supplies to American Marines who landed on Japanese-held Emirau Island in the St. Matthias group of the Southwest Pacific. An amphibious car pulls a truck ashore (left, centre), while in the background, troops form a chain in the surf to convey materials to the beach. US Marines captured the island on March 20, 1944, to complete encirclement of Japanese remnant garrisons on New Britain, New Ireland and the Northern Solomon Islands.**

D-Day

Preparations for the invasion of Occupied France had proceeded apace in Britain throughout the winter of 1943 and the spring of 1944. The Dieppe raid in 1942 had cost many lives, but it had also shown that it was going to be virtually impossible to capture and hold a major French port. 'Operation Overlord' was therefore planned to land on the less well-defended Normandy beaches to the east of the Cherbourg peninsula. This meant that a vast invading army would have to be both deployed and supplied without the advantages of a proper harbour, so artificial 'Mulberry' harbours were built to be towed across the English Channel to the landing beaches. In preparation for the invasion, special landing craft and amphibious vehicles were built, and large numbers of troops started assembling in southern Britain. In addition, a pipeline named 'PLUTO' was laid across the seabed from the Isle of Wight to Normandy to ensure this enormous army had enough oil supplies once the invasion was underway.

TOP: **American soldiers train for the Normandy landings. Barrage balloons were floated across the Channel to offer some protection against enemy aircraft.**

ABOVE MIDDLE: **General Eisenhower, Supreme Commander of the Allied invasion, plans 'Operation Overlord' from his headquarters in Britain.**

ABOVE: **A 'duck' is loaded onto its transport. These vehicles were ideal for seaborne invasions as they functioned both on land and water.**

ABOVE LEFT: **The American army trains for D-Day at Slapton Sands in Devon. The beach was selected for its similarity to Utah beach.**

MIDDLE LEFT: **General Eisenhower addresses camouflaged paratroopers just before they fly off on their mission to drop behind enemy lines in Normandy in the early hours of D-Day.**

LEFT: **The last items of equipment are loaded onto the transports ahead of D-Day.**

The landings

The overall commander, General Eisenhower, gave the order for the long-awaited attack on the Normandy beaches to begin on June 6, 1944: D-Day. Soon after midnight a vast invasion fleet of nearly 7,000 vessels closed in on the designated beaches, and parachutists and glider-borne troops landed behind German lines in Normandy. At first light, after an initial assault from thousands of aircraft, the invasion proper began.

Five beaches were designated for the landings; the Americans landed at the westernmost beaches, codenamed 'Utah' and 'Omaha', while the British, supported by the Free French, came ashore further east at 'Gold' and 'Sword' beaches. The landing at 'Juno', in the middle of the two British beaches, was undertaken by the Canadian military, under the command of the British.

By the end of the first day some 130,000 men had landed in Occupied France and were able to establish a bridgehead in Normandy. This had come at a cost of many lives, especially at Omaha beach, where the preliminary aerial bombardment had missed the German defences along the sea wall. As the Americans came ashore, the Germans fired relentlessly from their pillboxes, gunning down hundreds of men before the beach was finally taken.

ABOVE: An aerial view of Omaha beach on the morning of D-Day. Military vehicles attempt to exit the beach while small dots of men and beach obstacles can be seen in the water.

MIDDLE BELOW AND FAR LEFT: American troops come ashore in Normandy.

MIDDLE ABOVE: American soldiers await their fate in a 'Higgins Boat' as it approaches Omaha Beach.

TOP: Red Cross personnel and British infantry wade onto the beaches on 'D-Day+1', June 7, 1944.

BELOW: The Allied armada sets sail for Normandy in the early morning light of June 6, 1944.

DAILY MAIL, JUNE 7, 1944

The last act

June 6, 1944, will stand as one of the memorable days of all time. Upon this day was launched the greatest act of war in history - the invasion of Europe. This day saw well begun the campaign which will end the war in an Allied victory.

The Germans are beaten, and they begin to know it. Rome was one portentous symbol in their darkening sky. The Allies have the advantage in men, material, morale - everything. On the Eastern Front Russia awaits her moment. No secret weapon or tactical trick can save the Third Reich now.

This is the thought that must be uppermost in our minds as we watch unfolding the gigantic combined operation of the Allied land, sea, and air forces.

'The battle,' says Mr. Churchill, 'will grow constantly in scope and intensity for many weeks to come.' It will go well at one moment and not so well at the next. The fortunes of war will not always favour us.

After nearly five years of mingled triumph and disaster the British people are not likely to be led astray by excessive hope or unreasoning despair. Rather will they respond to the words of the King, who last night asked for a revival of the crusading spirit which sustained us in the dark days.

A great team

There have been warnings from high places. 'A long period of greater effort and fierce fighting lies ahead,' says President Roosevelt. General Eisenhower gives an inspiring Order of the Day to his troops, but, he says: 'Your task will not be an easy one.'

These warnings spring not from apprehension but from a just appraisal of the situation. They are based on the confidence so well expressed by General Montgomery: 'We are a great allied team.'

The mighty forces sweeping across the Channel are equipped with all the best that modern science and ingenuity can provide, and are trained to the last ounce. Supporting them is the terrifying punch of 11,000 war-planes, and transporting them are 4,000 large vessels, besides many thousands of smaller ones, backed by the power of six battleships and numerous other naval craft.

We can but marvel at the extent and intricacy of the operation. Beside these hosts of craft and myriad of aeroplanes, the record armadas of North Africa and Sicily become small.

According to plan

Of the actual fighting we know little, but things are going well. 'The operation is proceeding in a thoroughly satisfactory manner,' says Mr. Churchill, and nothing could be more emphatic. It may be that these landings are among the feints which the Prime Minister mentioned some weeks ago. The Germans appear to expect landings elsewhere. Let them speculate. We are content to wait on events.

Events are inspiring enough. The largest massed airborne landing yet attempted anywhere has been successfully made. Other troops have pushed several miles inland from the beaches.

There will be many conflicting reports in the next few days. Those which do not come from official sources or accredited correspondents should be treated with reserve.

The first three days will be the most critical. If our fine men, who carry with them all our thoughts and hopes, can establish themselves firmly during that time, the first big obstacle will have been victoriously overcome.

LEFT: A snapshot of Omaha beach after the initial landings hints at the vast scale of Operation Overlord. During D-Day, over 130,000 men were brought ashore in nearly 7,000 vessels.

TOP: German prisoners carry an injured comrade as they load onto boats destined for detention camps in Britain.

ABOVE MIDDLE: After facing down German guns, Allied soldiers had to contend with other parts of Germany's coastal defences. Mines and barbed wire were two such impediments which the advancing armies had to contend with.

BELOW MIDDLE: Troops start to move inland after securing a beachhead.

ABOVE: Wooden slat and wire runners are offloaded on the beaches. They were vital for getting the thousands of vehicles off the beaches.

Liberation of France

The Germans were not prepared for the invasion force to come ashore at Normandy. They had been fooled into believing that the attack would come along the coast near Calais by considerable decoy activity. Nevertheless the fighting was bitter and the men encountered stiff resistance across Normandy. Within a few days the Allies began linking up their five beachheads as ever more troops poured ashore. All the plans for increasing and supplying the invasion force worked and, on June 27, American forces captured the port of Cherbourg. On July 8 Caen was taken after fierce fighting and the Allies began to push out of Normandy towards Paris.

A second invasion force landed in the south of France near Toulon on August 15 and drove the Germans northwards along the Rhone valley. In all their advances the Allies were given invaluable assistance by the French Resistance, who harried the retreating Germans. The village of Oradour-sur-Glane in central France was to pay the price for increased resistance activity: members of the 2nd SS Reich Panzer division massacred the entire village on June 10 as they made their way to the front in Normandy.

Liberating troops finally reached Paris on August 24, where serious street fighting had erupted some days earlier. French troops under the command of General Leclerc were given the honour of being the first to enter the city. They were followed a day later by the leader of the Free French, General Charles de Gaulle, who was treated to a rapturous welcome, despite the residual threat of snipers.

ABOVE RIGHT: **Refugees hurry past an upturned German military vehicle and its dead driver in a Brittany village.**

MIDDLE RIGHT: **A French civilian takes her frustrations out on a German prisoner as he is marched through the streets of St-Mihiel at gunpoint.**

BELOW RIGHT: **French villagers watch as German prisoners are marched through the village of Ouistreham, on the Normandy Coast at 'Sword' Beach.**

RIGHT: **Eight days after D-Day, the leader of the Free French, General Charles de Gaulle, lands on the Normandy beaches.**

BELOW INSET: **A German soldier surrenders to the Allies days after the invasion.**

BOTTOM: **German POWs marched through Cherbourg by American troops.**

DAILY MAIL AUGUST 26, 1944
Germans in Paris surrender

THE battle for Paris is over. General Leclerc's tank columns broke into the capital early yesterday and in less than 12 hours' fighting smashed German resistance. The end came suddenly last evening when Leclerc, according to the Patriot radio, delivered an ultimatum to the general commanding the German garrison. The two, with the Maquis chief of Paris, then went to Montparnasse Station, where the terms of the capitulation were signed.

Under these, the German general at once ordered the cease fire. His men, unarmed, were to assemble at selected points to await orders. Their arms were to be piled and handed over intact.

At about the time Leclerc dictated his terms to the German, and while fighting was still in progress, General de Gaulle entered the city. Huge crowds greeted him with the 'Marseillaise' and cries of 'Vive de Gaulle!' to which he replied: 'I wish simply and from the bottom of my heart to say to you, Vive Paris!'

Later, in a broadcast to the people of Paris, General de Gaulle declared: 'France will take her place among the great nations which will organise the peace. We will not rest until we march, as we must, into enemy territory as conquerors.' De Gaulle said that France has the 'right to insist' that she shall never again be invaded by Germany.

TOP: De Gaulle makes his way through the crowds on the Champs Elysees in Paris.

ABOVE: French armoured divisions pass through the Arc de Triomphe in Paris.

RIGHT: German troops surrender to the Americans at Metz.

BELOW: The spire of Rouen Cathederal towers above a city in ruins.

The Liberation of the Low Countries

From France, the Allies raced into Belgium and liberated Antwerp and Brussels in the first week of September 1944. From Belgium, the Allies could have concentrated their forces on the industrial Ruhr region of Germany, but General Montgomery feared that an attack on the well-defended Siegfried Line would be too costly. Instead, he devised 'Operation Market Garden,' a plan to outflank the Siegfried Line through the Netherlands. His audacious operation involved dropping troops behind enemy lines to capture vital crossing points over a series of Dutch rivers and then following through with a swift ground invasion. The early stages were successful, but the British 1st Airborne Division met with strong German resistance at Arnhem on the Lower Rhine. The overland troops sent to relieve them were held up and then withdrawn, having sustained heavy casualties. Operation Market Garden was called off and the northern Netherlands remained under German control until the last months of the war. The Germans finally surrendered the country on May 5, 1945, just days before the end of the war.

ABOVE RIGHT: **Paratroopers get ready to jump from their plane behind enemy lines in Occupued Holland.**

MIDDLE RIGHT: **The Belgian Brigade, an independent infantry group formed in Britain, enter Brussels.**

RIGHT: **A soldier miraculously survives as a shell explodes right next to him at Arnhem.**

LEFT: **Allied paratroops deploy during Operation Market Garden.**

TOP LEFT: **British troops advance on Venray, a transport hub in the Netherlands.**

TOP RIGHT: **The British Second Army patrol through the Dutch town of Susteren.**

MIDDLE LEFT: **American troops help salvage possessions from homes set alight by the retreating Germans.**

MIDDLE RIGHT: **A smiling Belgian woman accompanies a British soldier as he marches a group of captured Germans through Antwerp.**

ABOVE: **German prisoners watch as British tanks pour into Belgium.**

BELOW: **British troops crawl from house to house through a Dutch village.**

DAILY MAIL SEPTEMBER 26, 1944

Arnhem front

Alexander Clifford, in a delayed cable, tells below the story of the first corridor battle.

The Germans have tried the obvious thing. They cut through our corridor behind us, and - if you like to put it that way - technically surrounded us.

The moment came at noon on Friday. It was a long time before anyone worked out exactly what happened. But the effective news was that German tanks and infantry were across our lines about 17 miles north of Eindhoven. All convoys must halt. The attack came from Germany itself. It may have been combined with an attempt to rescue some of the estimated 70,000 Germans who are partly cut off in Western Holland. Its main purpose was certainly to cut the axis.

From that moment the campaign abandoned all the rules again and became a series of personal adventures of each individual. For many truck drivers it meant sitting patiently by the roadside and listening to the firing ahead. For the men on the Arnhem front it meant the queer feeling that they were no longer fighting at the end of lines of supply but were temporarily in a military vacuum. For me it meant that I was cut off from my kit, which I had left in a little inn in the village where the Germans had attacked. It had been a gay, clean little inn, with an innkeeper who still managed to provide comfort and good Dutch food. And now the German mortars were falling on it.

Good humour

For the men on that section of the road it meant a sudden inferno of battle at a spot technically 30 miles behind our front lines. British and German trucks were blazing along the road and out into the fields. The possibility had been clearly enough foreseen. We always knew we could deal with anything of the sort if it occurred, and around Nijmegen there was a great deal of good-humoured banter as people who had been cut off began to go round trying to find billets for the night.

In the desert one would have joined some unit and slept in its laager. Here in civilised Europe one hardly knew what to do. In the end I and those with me decided to sleep on the billiards tables of a wayside pub. We ate sumptuously off German rations which we found in a train at Nijmegen railway station.

The night was a succession of wild alarms. Dutchmen, either honestly misinformed or deliberate Fifth Columnists, kept streaming in to tell us that the Germans were a mile away, that the British were evacuating Nijmegen, and so forth. None of it was remotely true. But the whole position was so unorthodox that it was understandable.

There was plenty of shooting during the night. But as often happens near the front, when morning came no one knew what it had been about. The only certain news was that the Germans were still across our path. Tanks had been sent to deal with them.

I followed down behind the leading patrol. It was necessary to reach that little inn quickly if any of my kit was to be saved. The Germans were reported to have been in the village itself for quite a few hours.

The ruptured stretch of axis was a trail of wrecked vehicles. It was almost like Normandy again, for the fields were strewn with dead cows. The tarmac was churned to dust where swerving tanks had ground it up. Half a dozen cottages along the way were still burning.

Methodical

While our patrol was still passing through all this we looked up and saw a new mighty phase of this three dimensional campaign. The sky filled fuller than I have ever seen it with planes and gliders. They came low, flying in steady and majestic patterns. They were simply reinforcements for the front. The Germans began to shoot at them. It was alarming to hear how near the Germans still were to the centre-line of our axis. They were firing from the nearest woods two fields away and their bullets were spangling the cloudy sky all round the great air fleet.

They got some hits. Extraordinarily few in the circumstances, but they could hardly help getting some. A towing plane began to burn and circled from the rest. Two or three gliders slipped loose and swung round towards what they knew were our lines.

But the Germans had given their positions away and firing broke out savagely once more from our land forces. A battle started chaotically among the fields and copses and farmhouses round about. It looked chaotic. But there was plenty of method in the way the Germans were being elbowed aside. You could piece it all together by watching the positions of the tanks along the roads and the places where the anti-tank guns were being dug in and the columns of smoke where our shells were falling.

And then we came to the gay, neat little village in whose inn we had left all our kit. Now it was empty and splintered and broken. It was grey with a pall of dust. Its streets were a tapestry of fallen branches and loose tiles and scattered bricks.

The inn itself was windowless and derelict. The innkeeper and his family were alive - they were down in the cellar steadfastly singing hymns. Almost everything they possessed was broken. Their yard was full of dead chickens. We dug what remained of our things out of the wreckage of our bedrooms. An American paratrooper came and told us to be quick about it, the village still wasn't very healthy.

Soviet advances in the east

The Soviet victory at Stalingrad in January 1943 marked a reversal of fortunes in the East. Within weeks the Red Army had liberated Kharkov and Kursk, but the Wehrmacht was not yet entirely on the defensive, and managed to recapture Kharkov one month later. In July 1943, Hitler launched an enormous offensive to retake Kursk and deal a resounding blow to the Red Army. 'Operation Citadel' as the attack was codenamed, was the largest tank battle in history, with more than 6,000 taking part in total. Despite suffering heavy losses, the Red Army won the battle and began an unrelenting march westward towards Berlin.

After Kursk, Soviet cities were liberated one after another; Kharkov was taken for the second time in August, followed by Smolensk in September and Kiev in November. The Soviet advance continued throughout early 1944, and by June, the Red Army had reached Belarus. Although the key to the Red Army's success was sheer manpower, it also benefited from a superior number of tanks and aircraft. Minsk fell on July 3 — along with 100,000 German prisoners— and by the end of the month they had advanced into eastern Poland. On October 1, with the Red Army just miles away, the residents of Warsaw rose up in rebellion against German rule. However, Stalin halted the Russian advance and left the fighters, who were largely anti-Communist, to their fate. German revenge was terrible and some 200,000 Poles died. When the Soviet Union did finally enter Warsaw in January 1945, it was far from the liberation that most Poles had hoped for.

Conspiracy against Hitler

With the Allies closing in on both fronts, it seemed that Germany's defeat might be within sight. This undoubtedly encouraged conspirators within the German army to go ahead with plans to assassinate the Führer. With Germany standing on the edge of an abyss, some German generals, who had always been lukewarm about Nazism, believed peace should be made with the Western Allies so the army could concentrate on keeping the Soviets from advancing on the Reich. One of the officers, Count von Stauffenberg, who was attached to Hitler's general staff, placed a bomb under a table at his headquarters in East Prussia on July 20, 1944. However, the bomb failed to kill Hitler and the conspirators were 'strung up like cattle' upon his orders.

The Siege of Leningrad

During the war Leningrad (St. Petersburg) was subjected to one of the longest sieges in modern history. The city was blocked-off by the German army from September 1941 until January 1943, during which time more than a million people died of starvation. The Soviets were able to get some supplies in and civilians out across Lake Ladoga, but convoys ran the gauntlet of German guns and millions remained trapped and starving inside the city. In January 1943, the Red Army launched Operation Iskra, a major offensive which punched a hole through the German siege lines within days. Fighting around the city continued for another year until the German army was forced to retreat in January 1944.

DAILY MAIL JANUARY 19, 1943

Leningrad free

The siege of Leningrad, second city of Russia, which has been blockaded by the German armies for more than 16 months, has been raised. Russian troops storming across the Neva River have smashed through the enemy's mighty defence zone and advanced 45 miles.

This tremendous news was given to the world in a special Moscow communiqué last night. A second special communiqué announced equally momentous successes on the southern front. Here Russian troops have crossed both the Donetz and Manych rivers - last great natural barriers protecting Rostov. Today the road to Rostov lies open. Thousands more prisoners have been taken on both these fronts; more towns captured in the North Caucasus, and the encircled German army at Stalingrad split in two.

South of Voronezh the enemy are falling back, abandoning their equipment and large quantities of supplies. Over 1,000 motor vehicles were captured intact on one stretch of road.

Here are the texts from the communiqués: A few days ago our troops concentrated south of Lake Ladoga launched an offensive against the German Fascist troops besieging Leningrad. They were given the task of destroying the enemy defences and thereby lifting the siege of Leningrad. It must be borne in mind that during the many months of the siege of Leningrad the Germans converted their positions on the approaches to the city into a strongly fortified area consisting of concrete emplacements and other fortifications.

The offensive of our troops was launched from two directions - from the western bank of River Neva, south-west and south-east of Schluesselburg, and from the east from the area south of Lake Ladoga. Having breached the enemy's defences, which extended to a depth of about nine miles, and having crossed the Neva, our troops in the course of seven days of severe fighting occupies the town of Schluesselburg. They also seized the large fortified points of Maryino Moskovskaya-Dubrobskaya, and Lipka; eight workers settlements and the railway stations of Sinyavino and Podgornaya.

Thus, after the first battles, the troops of the Volkhov and Leningrad fronts joined up on January 18, and broke through the investment of Leningrad. According to incomplete data our troops took prisoner 1,261 officers and men. In the course of the battle our artillery and mortars destroyed 470 fortified centres and block-houses, 25 strongly equipped observation posts, and 172 artillery and mortar batteries were silenced.

The break-through was carried out partly by the forces of the Leningrad front commanded by General Govorov and partly by the forces of the Volkhov front commanded by Army General Meretskov. Co-ordination of action of troops on both fronts was achieved by the representatives of Supreme Headquarters. Marshals of the Soviet Union Zhukov and Voroshilov.

Island-hopping

After securing Guadalcanal and New Guinea in 1943 the Americans continued with their offensives in the Pacific, jumping from island to island moving ever closer to Japan in a strategy known as 'island-hopping'. In the summer of 1944 the US liberated Saipan, Guam and Tinian in the Marianas Island chain, and the invasion of Peleliu and Angaur in the Palau island group followed shortly after. The capture of these islands helped put America's B-29 bombers within range of Japan's main island, and from June 1944 the US Army Air Force began a bombing campaign against Japanese cities with the intention of forcing the country into submission. In 1945 the bombing became relentless, especially in Tokyo, where thousands of people were killed in firebombing raids, but the Japanese government still refused to surrender.

TOP: In September 1944, US troops wade ashore almost unopposed on Morotai, one of the Moluccas Islands in the Dutch East Indies.

ABOVE: An American tank rolls through Garapan, the main city on Saipan island after the Japanese had been pushed out in July 1944.

ABOVE LEFT: Marines take cover as they meet with Japanese mortar fire on the beaches of Peleliu in the Palau island group.

LEFT: A long line of amphibious tanks come ashore at Tinian Island in the Marianas chain, August 1944.

BELOW: With the help of a jeep, US troops push an anti-tank gun ashore on the island of Angaur in the Palau group.

Battle for the Philippines

The United States had shared a close relationship with the Philippines ever since the islands were ceded to Washington at the end of the Spanish-American War of 1898. Thousands of American troops were in the Philippines when the Japanese invaded within hours of the attack on Pearl Harbor. Many were captured and, together with Filipino POWs, they were forced to endure an infamous death march to their internment camp in Bataan. The battle to liberate the Philippines from Japanese rule began on October 20, 1944 when US troops under the command of General Douglas MacArthur landed on the island of Leyte. The Japanese attempted to obstruct the landings in what became the largest naval battle of the entire war. The US scored a decisive victory, neutralizing the Japanese navy and allowing US and Australian forces to steadily recapture the Philippines. The Battle for Manila began in February 1945 and ended up being the only major urban battle fought in the Pacific campaign. Fighting was fierce and it took American soldiers more than one month to secure the city. By the time it fell on March 3, thousands of civilians had been killed and the city was almost utterly destroyed.

ABOVE: **An American soldier is carried by stretcher past the bodies of dead Japanese soldiers to a dressing station set up amid the debris of Manila city hall.**

LEFT: **An aerial view of the devastation caused during the fight for Manila. It was to be the only major urban battle of the Pacific campaign.**

BELOW: **Plumes of smoke rise above Manila during fierce fighting between US and Japanese forces in February 1945.**

Hitler's last stand

Although the Allies had made great strides through France and Belgium, Hitler would not accept the inevitability of defeat. A fresh offensive was planned in the Ardennes where the Allied line was weakest and his new 'wonder' weapons were ready to rain down a new terror upon London.

Battle of the Bulge

The German army launched its attack in the Ardennes in mid-December 1944. The plan was to split the Allied forces in two and create a corridor to the sea at Antwerp. The Allies managed to halt the advance on Antwerp, but not before it created a large bulge in the Allied line. The Wehrmacht found itself up against the might of the United States army and air force and by January the attack had waned. The attack only served to delay the Allied invasion of Germany temporarily and came at a cost of thousands of German lives.

TOP: Refugees flee from the Germans' December 1944 offensive in the Ardennes.

ABOVE MIDDLE: A small infantry group of the US 82nd Airborne ambush a German patrol near Bra in Belgium.

ABOVE: Allied troops cycle past damage done to the town of Bastogne during the German offensive.

ABOVE LEFT: German soldiers lie dead in the snow after attempting to storm Allied positions at Bastogne in Belgium during the 'Battle of the Bulge'.

LEFT: Members of the US Third Army, under the command of General Patton, advance on Houffalize in Belgium.

BELOW: The frozen body of a German soldier lies in the snow near Nefte. Many Germans questioned the wisdom of the Ardennes offensive, which cost many lives and diverted resources from the Eastern front.

'Wonder weapons'

In addition to his offensive in the Ardennes, Hitler had placed his faith in a new generation of secret weapons that would, he believed, inflict devastating damage on Britain. The first of these was the V1, a pilotless flying bomb, which began falling on London and South East England from June 1944. They caused casualties and heavy damage, as well as a dip in morale since most people had thought that the dangers of the Blitz had passed. They also somewhat helped Hitler reverse his rapidly declining popularity at home. Many Germans wanted retribution for the relentless Allied bombing campaign and Hitler's new weapon offered just that; the letter V was short for 'Vergeltung' the German word for revenge. The threat from the V1 decreased as the Allied troops overran the launch sites in northern France. Between June and early September, it is thought that almost 7,000 were launched; over half were destroyed before reaching their intended targets.

London came under attack from another German 'wonder' weapon, the V2, from September onwards. These, in contrast to the V1s, were long-range rockets and were fired from sites in places still controlled by the Nazis. The renewed threat from the skies revived the need to evacuate children from the threatened areas, and some 200,000 mothers and their children were forced to leave London. Nevertheless, Hitler's 'wonder weapons' were too little too late. Hitler had promised the German public great things from his 'wonder weapons', and when it became obvious that they would not alter the outcome of the war, the Nazis lost whatever public support they still had.

DAILY MAIL NOVEMBER 9, 1944

V2 Terror in London

Hour by hour last night Germany put out claims that V2 is causing widespread damage in London. Here, said radio spokesmen, was a long-range weapon more dangerous than V1. They said it had destroyed Euston Station, smashed a railway bridge, and devastated five named areas.

Goebbels seized on V2 as a morale builder to replace the anniversary celebrations of the Munich beer cellar putsch, abandoned this year for the first time.

The weapon - neutral sources have described it as a rocket-shell 'like a flying telegraph pole with a trail of flame behind it' - was said to have been in use for some weeks. But Berlin made no mention of it until yesterday.

First came a brief reference in the High Command's communiqué and then a spate of boosting radio reports and commentaries. Among all the claims there was one significant admission - that the launching of the 'deadly weapon' caused sacrifices 'among the crews.'

The Germans claimed to be in possession of full information of the damage caused by V2. 'The British Government,' said one radio spokesman, 'has so far concealed from its people

that a more effective, more telling, and therefore more dangerous long-range weapon has been in action in addition to the so-called flying bomb, which everyone knows about now.

'The German Command possess exact reports on the success and the effect of V2. If they required further proof of its accuracy, official British reports have supplied it by announcing, after nights in which London was exclusively attacked with V2, that flying bombs had again been over the capital.

'For the time being nothing further can be made known about the technical details of this missile. According to reports from England, the characteristic feature of the new weapon is that it cannot be heard or seen before its extraordinarily heavy detonation.'

Reports from Sweden and other neutral countries have credited V2 with a range of between 200 and 300 miles and a warhead of something under a ton of high explosive. Bases in Germany, Holland, Denmark, and Norway have been claimed as feasible for attacks on Britain. A rocket, it is said, would have to rise some 50 miles into the sky to achieve any considerable range, and it would travel at well over 700 miles per hour.

ABOVE LEFT: **A tragic image reveals the aftermath of a V-2 attack on the Belgian coast.**

ABOVE: **Rescue workers pull casualties from the wreckage caused by a V-2 bombing of Smithfield Market in London in April 1945.**

LEFT: **An anti-aircraft gun shoots down Hitler's 'wonder weapons' over Belgium.**

THIS PAGE & OPPOSITE: **This extraordinary sequence of photographs captures the chaos in the minutes following the devastating explosion of the V2 that fell on Smithfield, London. In the picture sequence opposite right, traders and other civilians work with police and ARP to release a casualty but it's clear there was nothing that could be done for this unnamed victim.**
The images on this page show the ironwork forming the roof and facade of the handsome Victorian building twisted beyond recognition and tangled in the rubble causing complications for the heavy rescue squad, seen at work with a crane (this page top).

Smithfield Market Destroyed

One of the worst V2 incidents of the Blitz was the devastation of Smithfield, London's historic meat and poultry market – an extensive enclosed indoor market at the corner of Farringdon Street and Charterhouse Street where the rocket landed. At 11.10 it was filled with buyers and sellers, while others were queuing outside to get in. The V2 fell out of the sky virtually destroying the crowded building, its blast making a crater that penetrated the railway tunnel and extensive sidings running below; the casualties, commodities and rubble mingled in a horrible melée. The decorative ironwork that formed the intricate facade collapsed in a tangle, making rescue work even more difficult. 110 people died immediately from the blast and many more were seriously injured.

Iwo Jima

On February 19, 1945 the 3rd, 4th and 5th divisions of the United States Marine Corps staged an amphibious invasion of Iwo Jima, an island some 700 miles south of Tokyo. The fighting was among the fiercest in the Pacific theatre, costing almost 7,000 American lives, making it the deadliest battle in the history of the US Marine Corps. Countless more Japanese died as they defended the island to the death, first engaging the marines in the open and later resisting from hiding place in caves. The battle ended on March 26, by which time 27 American servicemen had performed acts of bravery that would later win them the Medal of Honor.

TOP: The marines move up the beach under the shadow of the extinct volcano, Mount Suribachi.

ABOVE: Marines of the 4th Division storm the shores of Iwo Jima..

LEFT: An aerial view of the American invasion force approaching the shore of Iwo Jima, February 19, 1945.

BELOW: The American flag is raised on Mount Suribachi on February 23, 1945.

OPPOSITE ABOVE RIGHT: US marines attempt to flush Japanese soldiers out of a cave on Okinawa.

OPPOSITE MIDDLE RIGHT: Marines brace themselves as they detonate a satchel charge in a cave used by the Japanese to attack their positions on Okinawa.

OPPOSITE BELOW RIGHT: After capturing the Marianas islands in 1944, the US established several large military bases from where B-29 Superfortress bombers could attack the Japanese home islands.

OPPOSITE LEFT: Three marines kneel to pray in their fox holes in a rare quiet moment during the Iwo Jima campaign.

OPPOSITE BELOW: The cemetery of the Fifth Marine Division on Iwo Jima. Almost 7,000 American servicemen lost their lives in the battle for the island.

Okinawa

In mid-March as the Battle for Iwo Jima was drawing to a close, the US began the next offensive against the island of Okinawa. At just over 300 miles from Kyushu, the southernmost of Japan's four main islands, Okinawa was to be a springboard for the invasion of Japan proper. After a week long 'softening up' bombardment from the air, US troops of the Tenth Army came ashore largely unopposed. However, the Japanese were lying in wait at better-defended locations and the battle soon became a bloodbath. It took the US almost three months to wrestle control of the island and defeat the Japanese, who once again fought to the death. Unlike Iwo Jima, Okinawa had a large civilian population, which had been warned by Japanese propaganda not to expect any mercy from the Americans. Such scaremongering had terrible consequences; thousands of civilians committed suicide and thousands more died in the fighting. By the end of the battle an estimated 100,000 Japanese and 12,000 American servicemen had lost their lives.

Advancing through Germany

The early months of 1945 saw events moving fast, as the German will to fight on began to diminish. Throughout January the Russian armies advanced remorselessly upon the country from the east, liberating the Nazi concentration camp at Auschwitz on January 27. By now it was obvious to almost everyone involved that the final defeat of Germany was inevitable and imminent and Roosevelt, Churchill and Stalin met at Yalta in the Crimea to discuss the post-war division of Germany between February 4–11.

On April 14, the Red Army took Vienna and then turned its attention towards Berlin. The Russians crossed the Oder and two armies encircled Berlin on April 25. They joined to the west and then turned back towards the semi-ruined city, now devastated by artillery bombardment as well as by heavy bombing. Meanwhile the Allies were pushing on to the Rhineland and American troops captured the bridge at Remagen intact on March 7, at last establishing a much-needed bridgehead across the Rhine. Other Allied crossings were made and their forces now moved much further into Germany. American troops were just sixty miles from Berlin by 12 April.

DAILY MAIL MARCH 9, 1945

The Rhine crossed

We've done it. Early this morning strong infantry forces of General Hodge's American First Army are streaming across the Rhine into our newly won bridgehead on the east bank of the river. The final drive to meet the Russian armies in the heart of Germany - the last heave to end the war - has begun.

You can throw your hats in the air to-day. The success of our lightning stroke undoubtedly shortens the war by months. We are massing substantial forces in our rapidly expanding bridgehead 290 miles from Berlin.

This historic moment in the war came at 4.30 p.m. on Wednesday, when a spearhead task force of the First Army crossed the river in a sudden thrust which took the Germans completely by surprise. The crossing was made between Bonn and Coblenz. Opposition was light. Once on the other side the Americans spread out to get elbow-room. Then our main forces poured over. Before their tremendous onslaught the German defences cracked - then collapsed like a pack of cards.

More and more men swarmed across the river, and swiftly, efficiently, the bridgehead was built up.

OPPOSITE TOP RIGHT: Stalin and Roosevelt discuss the post-war settlement in Europe at the Yalta Conference in February 1945.

OPPOSITE MIDDLE RIGHT: Russian POWs show their gratitude to one of the American GIs who liberated their prison camp.

OPPOSITE BELOW RIGHT: Civilians in the German city of Rheydt, birthplace of Joseph Goebbels, cautiously emerge with white flags as the Americans approach.

OPPOSITE LEFT: American and Soviet troops link up for the first time at Torgau on the River Elbe on April 25, 1945.

OPPOSITE BOTTOM: While bridges were being constructed across the Rhine, thousands of paratroops were dropped into Germany by the largest airborne fleet ever assembled for a single mission. German civilians watch in amazement as the fleet, stretching some 500 miles, passes overhead.

TOP: Russian soldiers advance across open fields in Germany.

ABOVE LEFT: British troops pass the bodies of dead Germans as they move along the eastern bank of the Rhine.

ABOVE FAR LEFT: A fourteen-year-old boy is taken prisoner by the Allies. As the Allies closed in, Hitler futilely ordered that children help defend the Reich.

ABOVE: Winston Churchill crosses the Rhine with American troops and General Montgomery.

BELOW: As the German army retreated from the advancing Allies, they destroyed most of the bridges across the Rhine. Engineers had to build makeshift bridges so the Allies could cross into Germany.

YOU ARE NOW CROSSING THE RHINE RIVER THROUGH COURTESY OF 'E' CO. 17 ARMD. ENGR. BN. AND 'C' CO. 202 ENGR. C. BN.

The Holocaust

The Nazi regime subscribed to the belief that the German people sat atop of a global racial hierarchy and that other races – particularly Jews but also Gypsies and Slavs – were inferior and a threat to German racial purity. After they came to power in 1933, the Nazis began an incremental process of government-sponsored persecution against the country's Jewish population. They passed laws to deny Jews of their citizenship, to forbid them from marrying Aryans and to force them out of their jobs and businesses. The night of November 9, 1938, 'Kristallnacht', witnessed the first coordinated nationwide attack against Jews; many of Germany's synagogues were damaged and people were rounded up and sent to concentration camps. The following year, the war intervened and Germany's treatment of the Jews took an even deadlier turn.

ABOVE RIGHT: **Polish Jews are rounded up in Warsaw and marched to a concentration camp in March 1940.**

MIDDLE RIGHT: **German soldiers massacre Jews in newly-occupied Poland in retaliation for the death of a German soldier.**

BELOW RIGHT: **The Warsaw Ghetto burns as the Nazis try to suppress the uprising in April 1943.**

BELOW: **British soldiers liberated Belsen concentration camp on April 15. Thousands of people were found still alive but threatened by typhus, typhoid and dysentery, which were running rampant in the camp.**

Final Solution

From October 1939, as the Nazis consolidated their control of Poland, the country's large Jewish population was forced to live in walled-off ghettoes where thousands of people died of starvation and disease. After the invasion of the Soviet Union in June 1941, the Nazis began directly killing Jews using mobile killing units called 'Einsatzgruppen', which murdered more than one million men, women and children behind the German lines. In late 1941 the Nazis began constructing death camps and by early 1942 they had decided upon a 'Final Solution': the extermination of all the Jews of Europe. Millions of people were sent to death camps such as Auschwitz, Treblinka, Sobibor and Belzec, where they were murdered in specially designed gas chambers. The 'lucky ones' were sent to work camps, where they faced gruelling labour and death from disease, hunger and maltreatment. By 1945, as Allied soldiers closed in on the camps, thousands of inmates were moved by train or on forced 'death marches' to prevent them from being liberated and to prolong their suffering. By the time the war was over, more than six million Jews had lost their lives, which is an estimated two thirds of Europe's pre-war Jewish population.

In addition, the Nazis dehumanized, detained and murdered hundreds of thousands of other people deemed to be racially undesirable or politically unsound. These groups included gypsies, homosexuals and Communists, as well as people with physical or mental illnesses who were also subjected to forcible sterilizations as part of a campaign of so-called 'racial hygiene'.

ABOVE RIGHT: **A mountain of shoes belonging to the deceased inmates of Belsen are used for fuel.**

FAR RIGHT: **A snapshot of life around a water pump in a Nazi concentration camp after its liberation.**

RIGHT: **Josef Kramer, the 'Beast of Belsen', was the only senior officer remaining at the camp when it was liberated by the British. He was put on trial and hanged in December 1945.**

BELOW: **During 1945 the full extent of Nazi atrocities was slowly realized. Here shallow graves have been discovered** in woods ouside Luneburg, **Germany. A train on its way to Belsen stopped near the city and some prisoners were instructed to get out and bury those who had died in the overcrowded wagons during the journey. Those who dug the graves were shot dead by the guards and buried with the rest.**

DAILY MAIL MAY 9, 1945

VE Day - it's all over

London, dead from six until nine, suddenly broke into victory life last night. Suddenly, spontaneously, deliriously. The people of London, denied VE-Day officially, held their own jubilation. 'VE-Day may be tomorrow,' they said, 'but the war is over to-night.' Bonfires blazed from Piccadilly to Wapping.

The sky once lit by the glare of the blitz shone red with the Victory glow. The last trains departed from the West End unregarded. The pent-up spirits of the throng, the polyglot throng that is London in war-time, burst out, and by 11 o'clock the capital was ablaze with enthusiasm.

Processions formed up out of nowhere, disintegrating for no reason, to re-form somewhere else. Waving flags, marching in step, with linked arms or half-embraced, the people strode down the great thoroughfares - Piccadilly, Regent-street, the Mall, to the portals of Buckingham Palace.

They marched and counter-marched so as not to get too far from the centre. And from them, in harmony and discord, rose song. The songs of the last war, the songs of a century ago. The songs of the beginning of this war - 'Roll out the Barrel' and 'Tipperary'; 'Ilkla Moor' and 'Loch Lomond'; 'Bless 'em All' and 'Pack Up Your Troubles.'

ABOVE RIGHT: **VE Day in London.** Thousands gather for celebrations in Trafalgar Square.

RIGHT: **VE Day in Moscow.** Aircraft searchlights are used to light up the night sky.

BELOW: **VE Day in New York.** Thousands of people pour into Times Square in celebration of Germany's unconditional surrender.

Victory in Europe

By mid-April 1945, Russian troops were fighting their way through Berlin street by street, heading towards the Reichstag. Hitler had ordered 'fanatic determination' from all Germans in the defence of Berlin. However, he retreated to his underground bunker on April 16 and began to lose his grip on reality. On April 30, after nominating Admiral Karl Doenitz as his successor and blaming the Jews for the war, Hitler and his new wife Eva Braun committed suicide. On the same day, above ground, the battle for Berlin was won and the Soviet flag fluttered atop the ruins of the Reichstag building. The following day Hitler's propaganda minister Joseph Goebbels and his wife supervised the deaths of their six children before killing themselves. The remains of the German armies now began to surrender and, on May 7, General Eisenhower formally accepted the unconditional surrender of Germany. VE Day was celebrated across the world the following day, but the world was not yet at peace.

ABOVE RIGHT: **Street parties were held in towns and villages across Britain. Five and a half years of war had taken its its toll on the British public, and shortages and rationing would continue for several years.**

ABOVE FAR RIGHT: **Revellers pile onto a van as it drives through the crowds in Parliament Square, London, on VE Day.**

RIGHT: **With Britain and America pounding the city from above, and the Soviets attacking on the ground, Berlin is left as a shell of its former self.**

ABOVE: **The Soviet Union holds its official victory parade in Red Square, Moscow, on June 24.**

BELOW: **The Reichstag, the symbolic heart of Berlin, lies in ruins after the war.**

Victory in Japan

While victory was being celebrated in Europe, the war against Japan was still raging, but here too the Allies were pushing steadily forward. British forces finally liberated Burma from Japanese control on August 2, 1945, and the American push through the Pacific was bringing US troops gradually closer to Japan.

Roosevelt had died suddenly on April 12 and the new President, Harry Truman, was confronted with the challenging task of winning the war in the Far East. In July 1945, America successfully tested the first nuclear device and it was up to Truman to decide whether this potentially devastating piece of military technology should be used in the Pacific theatre. Truman realized how costly an invasion of the Japanese mainland would be; he had been given a foretaste when an estimated 12,000 Americans died taking Okinawa Island in March. He was also aware that the Allies were exhausted and that many people had lost focus on the Pacific campaign amid the jubilation of the victory in Europe. In addition, the Soviet Union was preparing to declare war on Japan and Truman was keen to stem Stalin's influence in the region. All these considerations encouraged Truman to take the momentous decision to use the bomb.

BOTTOM: The scene as troops of the Australian Seventh Division landed east of the Japanese–held Borneo port of Balikpapan, a great oil centre, supported by American ships and aircraft.

TOP RIGHT: Australian forces begin their seaborne landings on the island of Tarakan, Borneo on May 1, 1945. The invasion was well-executed, though there were problems in landing; the Allies had overwhelming numbers by comparison with the Japanese garrison because fierce resistance was expected. Tarakan's oilfields were strategically important and the Allies hoped to make good use of the island's airfield. This picture shows the effectiveness of the modified landing craft that were equipped with rockets; these LCMRs could deliver devastating barrages with lightning speed, just before attacking infantry landed. Pockets of Japanese soldiers held out until June 21.

TOP LEFT: A Japanese tank trap on the beach at Tarakan Island, off the East Coast of Borneo, snares an Australian light tank. Aussie engineers of the Ninth Australian Imperial Forces division try to free it with another tank. A landing craft in the background is made ready to disgorge its valuable cargo.

ABOVE LEFT AND RIGHT: Irrawaddy rail-head town, Prome, was liberated after a sharp encounter with a few straggling Japanese who held on while the bulk of their troops in the district were wandering aimlessly and defeated around the wild country south of the town. Allied armoured vehicles on the road to Prome were held up by a river crossing.

BELOW: Fort Drum, nicknamed the Concrete Battleship, was a defensive installation built on a tiny island in Manila Bay to cover its approaches and the US garrison of Corregidor. The heavily fortified installation bristled with guns and fought hard to resist the Japanese who took it in 1942. When Allied forces recaptured Corregidor in February 1945, Fort Drum remained in the control of the Japanese until April 13 when US forces approached, avoided its heavy guns and landed. A landing craft tanker was called into use and several thousand gallons of an inflammable mixture were poured into the ventilation system and TNT charges set, creating an explosive inferno that wrecked the fort and killed its garrison. In this remarkable photograph, taken by Acme War Pool Correspondent, Stanley Troutman, the LCM can be seen in the foreground while infantry cover the engineers who are feeding the fuel into the vents and setting their charges.

ABOVE LEFT: While conflict subsided in the European and Mediterranean theatres of war, the Allies remained engaged in fierce and deadly combat with Japan in the Far East. Australian troops were fighting in the jungle of New Guinea under the most difficult conditions resulting in many casualties.

ABOVE MIDDLE: Ready for emergency a Bren-gunner takes cover alongside the track of the Western Railway at Labuan Island, Borneo to cover the advance of the 9th Division Infantry.

ABOVE RIGHT: A feature of the naval operations off the Sakashima Islands in support of the Okinawa landings was the Japanese suicide aircraft attack. Here, firefighters are busy on board one of H.M. carriers of the British Pacific Fleet after a Japanese suicide plane had crash landed on the flight deck.

LEFT: Australian soldiers pass the corpse of a dead Japanese soldier killed in the gateway leading to a plantation property on Labuan Island, Borneo.

Ultimate weapon unleashed on Japan

An outcome of the Potsdam Agreement was the Potsdam Declaration which set out the terms for Japan's unconditional surrender. These were sent to the Japanese government by Truman, Churchill and China's President Chiang Kai-shek on July 26. The Japanese government adopted a policy of ignoring the ultimatum because it took away all Japanese sovereignty and reduced its territories as well as threatening the prosecution of war crimes. The response was delivered indirectly by the Japanese Prime Minister in a press conference. The ultimatum was uncompromising in guaranteeing the total devastation of Japan if it did not surrender, but the Imperial forces had no knowledge of the atomic bomb and had already withstood strategic bombing that had destroyed vast areas of some of its cities; the military would rather fight to the death than surrender and leave the Emperor at the mercy of foreign powers.

LEFT: The Allied powers called time on the Japanese and sent three B 29 bombers, one of them the Enola Gay, equipped with the 'Little Boy' nuclear device to bomb Hiroshima on August 6, followed by 'Fat Man' dropped on Nagasaki on August 9. The world suddenly became acquainted with the awesome weapon that would dominate military and political reality for generations to come, symbolised in the terrifying mushroom cloud, photographed here over Nagasaki.

LEFT INSET: The casing of an atomic bomb of the same type as 'Fat Man', on display in the USA.

TOP: Directly under the Hiroshima hypocentre was a modern ferro-concrete building which was one of the few that remained standing after the blast. A dazed survivor wanders the scorched streets of Hiroshima. In the months and years to come the survivors continued to die, many of them from terrible burns and horrible radiation sickness.

ABOVE: Nagasaki razed to the ground.

City of 300,000 vanishes

Hiroshima, Japanese city of 300,000 people, ceased to exist at 9.15 on Monday morning. While going about its business in the sunshine of a hot summer day, it vanished in a huge ball of fire and a cloud of boiling smoke - obliterated by the first atom bomb to be used in the history of world warfare.

Such is the electrifying report of the American crew of the Super-Fortress which dropped the bomb as a cataclysmic warning to the Japs to get out of the war or be destroyed. Hiroshima, the whole crew agreed, was blotted out by a flash more brilliant than the sun.

They told their astonishing story here at Guam to-day. The explosion, they said, was tremendous and awe-inspiring. The words 'Oh my God' burst from every man as they watched a whole city blasted into rubble. Although they were ten miles away from the catastrophe, they felt the concussion like a close explosion of A.A. fire.

The men had been told to expect a blinding flash. They wore special black goggles. Only three of them knew what type of bomb was being dropped. 'It was hard to believe what we saw.' That was how Col. Paul W. Tibbits, pilot of the Super-Fort, described the explosion.

He said: 'We dropped the bomb at exactly 9.15 a.m. and got out of the target area as quickly as possible to avoid the full effect of the explosion. We stayed in the target area two minutes. The smoke rose to a height of 40,000ft.

'Only Captain Parsons, the observer; Major Ferebee, the bombardier; and myself knew what was dropped. All the others knew was that it was a special weapon. We knew at once we had got to get the hell out of there. I made a sharp turn in less than half a minute to get broadside to the target.

'All of us in the plane felt the heat from the brilliant flash and the concussion from the blast. 'Nothing was visible where only minutes before there was the outline of a city, with its streets and buildings and piers clearly to be seen. 'Soon fires sprang up on the edge of the city, but the city itself was entirely obscured.'

TOP RIGHT: **The trio of planes flying towards Hiroshima on August 6 was picked up by Japanese radar and judged to be a reconnaissance flight so no defensive measures were taken. At around 8.15 am, the Little Boy nuclear device exploded about 2,000 feet above the target area in central Hiroshima creating a blaze of light and a shock wave that killed an estimated 70,000 citizens instantly and demolished all of the traditionally constructed buildings in range. In the Enola Gay, co-pilot Robert Lewis asked the question that would be repeated around the world: 'My God, what have we done?'**

MIDDLE RIGHT: **Both Hiroshima and Nagasaki, though they were important cities for military reasons, were relatively untouched by strategic bombing,** which enabled the Manhattan Project's researches to continue in 'real' conditions. Tokyo, pictured, was not so unscathed - fire-bombing had already destroyed vast areas of the capital. The Allies avoided fire-bombing Kyoto but many other Japanese cities such as Nagoya were also devastated, fire-bombs destroying the many wooden buildings, rich with Japan's cultural and religious heritage.

BELOW: **A selection of newspapers from across the United States during the week of the bombings.**

RIGHT: **The devastated city of Tokyo is pictured from the heavily-defended US embassy in September 1945.**

The big three at Potsdam

The Potsdam Conference was held at Cecilienhof, the home of Crown Prince Wilhelm Hohenzollern, in Potsdam, occupied Germany, from 17 July to 2 August 1945. Participants were the Soviet Union, the United Kingdom, and the United States. The three nations were represented by Communist Party General Secretary Joseph Stalin, Winston Churchill and US President Harry S. Truman. They gathered to decide how to administer punishment to the defeated Nazi Germany, which had agreed to unconditional surrender nine weeks earlier, on May 8, 1944. The goals of the conference also included the establishment of post-war order, peace treaties issues, and countering the effects of war.

ABOVE LEFT: **A London policeman is held aloft by military men from the US and New Zealand in celebration of VJ Day.**

LEFT: **This was the scene in Piccadilly at three o'clock in the morning. Celebrations for VJ Day were, if anything, even more unrestrained than those for VE Day. It was the end to a war which for people in Britain had lasted just twenty days short of six years.**

ABOVE: **Service men and women celebrate in Piccadilly.**

TOP: **The Potsdam Conference was held at Cecilienhof, the home of Crown Prince Wilhelm Hohenzollern, in Potsdam, occupied Germany, from 17 July to 2 August 1945. Participants were the Soviet Union, the United Kingdom, and the United States. The three nations were represented by Communist Party General Secretary Joseph Stalin, Winston Churchill and**

US President Harry S. Truman. They gathered to decide how to administer punishment to the defeated Nazi Germany, which had agreed to unconditional surrender nine weeks earlier, on May 8, 1944. The goals of the conference also included the establishment of post-war order, peace treaties issues, and countering the effects of war.

VJ Day Celebrations

Victory in Japan was made official on August 15 and London came to a standstill as celebrations began in earnest. By coincidence, it was also the State Opening of Parliament and the King and Queen's horse-drawn carriage ride to Westminster turned into an impromptu victory parade. In Trafalgar Square a fountain became part of the victory parade!

ABOVE: **The Royal Family on the balcony at Buckingham Palace.**

FAR LEFT: **The crowds gathered in Trafalgar Square on VJ Day - everyone had their own way of celebrating!**

LEFT: **Eisenhower returns to a hero's welcome as crowds throng Broadway in New York City in the hope of seeing the general.**

BELOW: **People throng London streets on August 11 as news of the defeat, if not surrender, of Japan filters through.**

Peace

On July 17, 1945 the Allied leaders met at Potsdam near Berlin. Churchill and Stalin met with the new US President, Harry Truman, and during the conference, Churchill was replaced with Clement Attlee, the new British Prime Minister. He had defeated Churchill in a General Election on July 5 with the promise of nationalizing major industries and introducing a welfare state. At Potsdam, the Allied leaders agreed that Germany would be disarmed, 'de-nazified' and divided into four zones of occupation, controlled by Britain, the United States, the Soviet Union and France.

'Iron Curtain'

A final peace agreement was never signed and the Second World War soon gave way to the Cold War. The erstwhile Allies could not agree on the post-war make-up of Europe because of the ideological gulf between them. In southern and western Europe, Britain and America promoted democracy, free trade and anti-Communism, while in Eastern Europe, the Soviet Union imposed centrally planned economies and Communist governments. According to Winston Churchill an 'iron curtain' had descended across Europe. A final resolution to the Second World War in Europe would elude the world until after the fall of the Berlin Wall and the collapse of Communism at the end of the 1980s.

In the Pacific theatre a peace treaty was more forthcoming. Japan was placed under American military occupation from 1945 until 1952. In the early 1950s, the United States had to turn its attention to the war in Korea and sought a peace treaty with Japan. The Treaty of San Francisco was signed in September 1951, officially ending the War in the Pacific when it came into effect the following April.

ABOVE RIGHT: **Japan signs its official surrender to the British in Burma on September 12, 1945.**

ABOVE: **Churchill met British military commanders at Berlin airport when he arrived for the Potsdam conference which started on July 15. The conference continued until the end of the month but by that time Churchill was no longer British Prime Minister. Immediately after the victory** against Germany, the coalition government he had led since 1940 was dissolved and a new election called. Churchill's Conservative party suffered a shock defeat as Labour won a landslide victory in a country eager for change. The Labour Prime Minister, Clement Attlee, replaced Churchill at Potsdam.

RIGHT: **In July 1945, the three major Allied powers met again at Potsdam in an attempt to** sort out the fine details of the peace process in Europe. The handshake here is the first meeting of Prime Minister Churchill with Harry S. Truman, the new American President. Tragically, President Roosevelt had died unexpectedly on April 12, 1945, less than a month before Germany's unconditional surrender and as Vice-President, Truman was sworn in.

BELOW: On a visit to Berlin Churchill rests in a chair that was said to have been in the bunker in which Hitler committed suicide.

LEFT: When the Japanese signed the Allied surrender terms aboard the USS Missouri in Tokyo Bay, HMS Duke of York, flagship of Admiral Sir Bruce Fraser, Commander-in-Chief of the British Pacific Fleet, was alongside. Here, the Japanese interpreter who accompanied the pilot is searched upon his arrival aboard H.M.S. Duke of York.

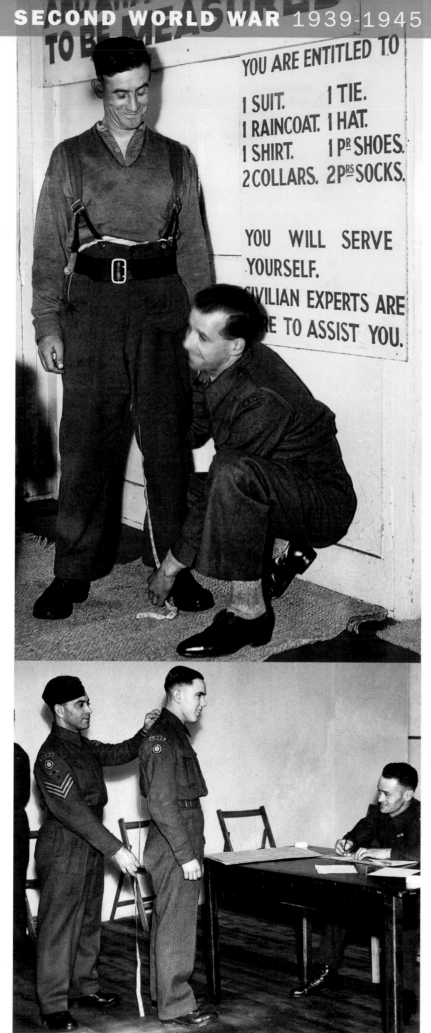

YOU ARE ENTITLED T.O

1 SUIT.   1 TIE.
1 RAINCOAT. 1 HAT.
1 SHIRT.   1 PR SHOES.
2 COLLARS. 2 PRS SOCKS.

YOU WILL SERVE
YOURSELF.
CIVILIAN EXPERTS ARE
RE TO ASSIST YOU.

FAR LEFT: Private H. Salter, being measured here, is the first man to claim a 'non-austerity discharge suit'. Austerity Regulations had come into effect in March 1942. Clothing styles which used valuable materials merely for show were not permitted; so double-breasted jackets, turn-ups on trousers and decorative buttons were banned. By the time Private Salter was ready for discharge in October 1944, the war was going well enough for the regulations to be relaxed.

LEFT: A happy Private Salter with his complete 'demob' outfit.

BOTTOM LEFT: Being measured for a 'demob' suit. Many men had been in service for the duration of the war and had not acquired any new civilian clothing for years. Their clothing entitlement was outlined in a poster in the demobilisation centre.

BELOW AND BOTTOM: Scenes like this were repeated for the thousands of service personnel returning to 'civvy street.'

REMEMBER IN FUTURE YOU MAY HAVE TO USE COUPONS CHOOSE WISELY PLEASE DON'T HURRY IN YOUR CHOICE

Demobilising the armed forces

Nine million American men and women had enlisted in the United States Armed forces during World War II. Following the Axis surrenders, troops were deployed to Japan and Germany to occupy the two defeated nations. Two years after World War II, the Army Air Forces separated from the Army to become the United States Air Force.

At the start of the Second World War the British Army Strength stood at 897,000 men including reserves. By the end of 1939, the strength of the British Army stood at 1.1 million men, and further increased to 1.65 million men during June 1940. By the end of the war and the final demobilisations in 1946, over 3.5 million men had been enlisted in the British Army.

ABOVE: **German prisoners of war who have been attending divine service at Somerton Parish Church near Bury St. Edmunds, photographed at choir practise. They sing their hymns from pencilled carbon copies from a German book.**

ABOVE RIGHT: **Sgt Arthur Freund receives his Honourable Discharge, which gave him the thanks of a grateful nation, a substantial cash payment, a service badge for his jacket and his discharge papers. A grand total of 11 million service personnel would follow in his footsteps.**

BELOW: **Axis POWs are put to work by British forces running feeding centres.**

RIGHT: **The smiles of these recently demobilised men speak louder than words.**

Living in peace

The end of the war brought enormous relief to the many that survived in its shadow but left millions displaced, bereaved, wounded, scarred psychologically or awaiting release from prison - or the serving of a sentence in the courts of justice assembled by the victors. Some German prisoners had been transported across the Atlantic to labour for the war effort; many of them were content to stay in the countries that had imprisoned them, knowing the deprivations in their native land.

The rubble of Berlin had to be cleared and the civilians of the city set about creating some order, but there was much suffering as the German economy was shattered, the people dazed and afraid of the occupying troops. Food was scarce in Germany and the typical ration for German civilians left many close to starving. However, those that were willing to work, particularly those involved in heavier duties such as construction, fared much better and were paid well enough to supplement their rations, while aiding the reconstruction of their cities.

LEFT AND BELOW: **Berliners, mainly women, work in chain gangs to clear rubble from bomb-sites.**

FAR LEFT: On traffic duty at the Brandenburg Gate is a 22-year-old Russian woman soldier, Feodora Bondenko, who had marched from Kiev with Marshal Zhukov's forces.

LEFT: At a bend in the Kurfürstendamm, in front of the Kaiserin Augusta Gedächtniskirche scarred by Allied bombing, two Berlin women pass by a Russian signpost.

BELOW: A crowd of Berliners wait for a bus in a street just off Potsdamer Platz. Buses were one of the few ways for citizens to get around the city but the service was severely curtailed. Life for the defeated citizens was harsh. They had to set about trying to clear up the wreckage, as much rubble and a damaged vehicles still littered the street. Food, clean water and shelter were all in short supply.

The Nuremberg trials

Once the war was over, there was widespread agreement that the Nazi leaders should be brought to trial as war criminals. Some of them had escaped in the confusion of the final days of the war, and others, like Goebbels and Hitler himself, had avoided retribution for their actions by committing suicide. Those who had been captured were brought before an International War Crimes Court. This met at Nuremberg in November 1945 and sat for several months, during which time it considered enormous amounts of evidence and heard very many witnesses. Of the twenty-one defendants, three were acquitted, seven received prison sentences ranging from ten years to life and the remainder were sentenced to death. The most notable among those to be executed were Field Marshal Göring and Joachim von Ribbentrop, the German Foreign Minister. Hours before he was due to be hung, Göring committed suicide by swallowing a cyanide capsule which he had managed to keep hidden, but on October 16, 1946 the executions of the others took place. Their bodies, together with that of Göring, were taken to Munich to be cremated and, according to the official announcement, their ashes were 'scattered in a river somewhere in Germany'.

LEFT: The defendants listen to the summing-up.

ABOVE: Rudolf Hess (left) and Joachim von Ribbentrop during a mealtime at the Nuremberg courthouse.

BELOW: Prisoners in the dock during the Nuremberg trials. Göring is on the far left.

The World's Biggest Conflict

When the largest conflict the world had ever known finally came to an end, it had claimed the lives of an estimated 55 million people, the majority of whom were civilians. Some 20 million Russians, 10 million Chinese and 6 million European Jews, who were never part of the 100 million mobilised to fight, are believed to have perished. Modern warfare had been characterised by the employment of advanced technologies, which had led to the deaths of civilians across the globe, and had culminated in the use of the atomic bomb, the threat from which continues to overshadow our existence to this day.

LEFT: Celebratory fireworks make a spectacular display in the night sky over the River Thames giving a suitable climax to Victory Day.

BELOW: Many Allied service personnel lay buried close to where they fell, killed in action. Few sights are more stirring and sad than the serried ranks of

headstones in these haunting places that mark the heroism of those who gave their lives in the face of inhuman conflict. Here on Iwo Jima, in the US Cemetery of the Fifth Marine Division lie nearly 7,000 American servicemen who died in the capture of this tiny island that

became so symbolic to the world.

ABOVE: On June 16, 1948 a ceremony took place in Cardiff as the remains of over 4,000 American soldiers, most killed during the D-Day landings, were carried onboard the USS Lawrence Victory bound for New York.

Acknowledgements

The photographs in this book are from the archives of the Daily Mail.
Particular thanks to Steve Torrington, Alan Pinnock and all the staff.

Thanks also to Alison Gauntlett, Lauren Oing, Michael Quiello, Bradford Swann,
Laurence Socha, Christopher Sullivan, Patricia Annunziata,
Caitlin Gildea, Cliff Salter, Alice Hill, Jill Dorman and Richard Betts

Dedication
For Eric McDonald Good